TEACHING PREACHING

D1551328

Teaching Preaching

Isaac Rufus Clark
and
Black Sacred Rhetoric

KATIE GENEVA CANNON

continuum

NEW YORK • LONDON

BV
4211.3
.C36
2007

2007

The Continuum International Publishing Group Inc
80 Maiden Lane, New York, NY 10038

TheContinuum International Publishing Group Ltd
The Tower Building, 11 York Road, London SE1 7NX

Printed in the United States of America

Library of Congress Cataloging-in-Publication Data

Cannon, Katie G.
    Teaching preaching : Isaac Rufus Clark and Black sacred rhetoric / Katie Geneva Cannon.
      p. cm.
    Includes bibliographical references and index.
    ISBN-13 978-0-8264-1441-0 (hardcover : alk. paper)
    ISBN-10 0-8264-1441-9 (hardcover : alk. paper)
    ISBN-13 978-0-8264-2897-4 (paperback : alk. paper)
    ISBN-10 0-8264-2897-5 (paperback : alk. paper)
    1. Preaching. 2. Clark, Isaac Rufus. I. Title.
BV4211.3 .C36 2002
251—dc21

                              2002011126

For
my loving father,
Esau Cannon,
who believes
women have as much right to send people to hell as men do

For
my wise friend,
Joan Dexter Blackmer,
who knows
the cost of the round dance

For
my bestest friend,
Angelin Jones Simmons
who preaches
from make do to must do more

In grateful memory of
Dr. Isaac Rufus Clark, Sr.,
who teaches
never tamper with people's souls

Contents

Acknowledgments

T HE WRITING OF THIS BOOK has taken place over the course of a dozen years. Therefore, I must begin by thanking my editor, Frank Oveis, for his commitment to this project.

I owe a debt of gratitude to my classmates who walked this life-transforming journey with me in the year-long homiletics course in 1972–1973 at the Interdenominational Theological Seminary in Atlanta, Georgia. I benefited from the sacred prayer-timber that the following persons offered up as Dr. Isaac R. Clark developed our ethical consciousness in African American sacred rhetoric: Larry Hill, Lonnie Oliver, Aaron A. Bush, Jr., Anthony Williams, Portia D. Hewlett Lacy, Jacquelyn Grant, Jerry Woodfork, James Wilbourn, Clayton Taylor, Littleton Price, Curtis Bines, Glenn Anderson, Conrad Pridgen, Patrick Frazier, Steve Hassmer, Tommy Davis, Bennie Mitchell, Lawrence McKinney, Kenneth Fisher, and William C. Davis. Extremely helpful was the knowledge gained from our chief teaching assistants, Lloyd Green, Jr., John A. King, Willie James Christian, and Adam J. Richardson.

Special mention must be made of Minnie J. Wright, Julius McDowell, Edward McDowell, Jr., Karen Y. Collier, Cleopatrick Lacy, Sidney Locks, Alison P. Gise Johnson, Boykin Sanders, Stacey M. Floyd-Thomas, Valerie E. Dixon, C. Michelle Venable-Ridley, David Mussatt, Clinton Brantley, Carolyn L. McCrary, Deborah McDowell, Randall Bailey, Spencer C. Gibbs, H. Samuel Johnson, Antonio Lawrence, Arthur Canada, Elijah Freeman, Jacquelyn Alexander, Joseph Washington, Jerry L. Kincaid, A. Clark Jenkins, Telley Gadson, Larry McCutcheon, Clarence S. Wallace, Vivian P. McFadden, Gloria J. Tate, Joe S. Ratliff, Dorothy Exume, Rosetta E. Ross, Ernest Augcomfar, Chester Jones, Emma I. Darnell, Sujay Johnson Cook, Theresa Bredell Sahou, Bridgette

Hector, John W. Kinney, Kerry L. Haynie, and Sonia Sanchez. Each stirs my creative imagination and encourages me to live in solidarity as a prophetic witness.

Appreciation is offered to Dr. Betty J. Watkins Clark. Without my conversation with her during the Consultation on Black Preaching in Commemorative Celebration of the Life and Labors of Dr. Isaac R. Clark in November 1990, this book would never have come to fruition.

Acknowledgment is here given to Drs. James H. Costen, Melva W. Costen, Oswald P. Bronson, Charles B. Copher, Thomas Hoyt, Jr., Kenneth E. Henry, G. Murray Branch, John C. Diamond, Leonard C. Lovett, Cecil Cone, Wilson N. Fleminister, Rudolph Obey, Jonathan Jackson, Raymond Worsley, Ndugu Ofori-atta-Thomas, Robert Osborn, Mance Jackson, Gayraud S. Wilmore, Robert T. Newbold, Marsha Snulligan Haney, Oliver J. Haney, Jr., Riggins R. Earl, Jr., David L. Wallace, and Bobby Joe Saucer. They continue to open my eyes to God's grace in the running of life's race.

I am indebted to all of the students and workshop participants over the past twenty-eight years who studied these notes in their roughest forms and offered constructive suggestions as they learned to preach using the I. R. Clark homiletical method. Most recently, they include Jeanette A. Bethea, Steven Blunt, James Coe, Delano Douglas, Linda Gilliam, Jennifer McGill, Devon Musson, Terry Pasco, Stacie Pitts, Sharon Garlington, Reginald William, Jr., Stacey Edwards, Raymond Reid, Kathryn Van Brocklin, and Richelle White.

I would like to use this opportunity to thank my current colleagues at Union Theological Seminary–The Presbyterian School of Christian Education and members of the Pan-African Seminar on Religion and Economics in Africa and the Diaspora, as well as my former colleagues and friends at Temple University, the Episcopal Divinity School, New York Theological Seminary, Covenant United Presbyterian Church, First African Presbyterian Church, the Presbyterian Church of the Ascension, and the Presbyterian Church of the Master in New York City.

The staff at the Robert W. Woodruff Library in the Atlanta University Center, the Charles H. Blockson's Afro-American Collection at Temple University in Philadelphia, and the William Smith Morton Library at Union Theological Seminary-PSCE in Richmond were generous with their professional services. Pam Austin, Vanessa Piggott, and Patsy Verreault were particularly helpful in assisting me in my research needs.

Members of my nuclear and extended family continue to provide a cool drink of water from home. Although it is not possible to mention everyone individually, I thank Deacon Leroy Jones and Ms. Elsie Pinnacle Jones in Ladson, South Carolina. Their generous hospitality and words of wisdom have had a lasting impact on my spiritual formation.

In addition, I am particularly grateful to my mother, Corine Lytle Cannon; my sisters, Sara Cannon Fleming, Doris Cannon Love, Sylvia Moon Edwards; and my brothers, James Ernest Cannon, John Wesley Cannon, and Jerry Lytle Cannon, whose practical advice continues to enrich my mind and nourish my soul.

I would also like to thank the Cannons—Bridgett, Tyrone, Wesley, Rudolph, Raymond, Rosalynn, Richard, James, Nicholas, Caleb, Gabriel, Reuben, and Javon; the Flemings—Sylvester, Sarbeth, Emanuelette, Jerome, Joshua, Isaiah, Samuel; the Moons—Etta, Tracey, and Christopher; the Loves—Cedric and Courtney; the Daniels—Phyllis, Thomas, and Joshua; the Wilsons—Kim and Greg; and the Lindseys—Tammy, Theo, and Tirara. Their love and laughter offer glimpses of the commonwealth of God.

Above all, I am indebted to the three people to whom this book is dedicated—Esau Cannon, Joan Dexter Blackmer, and Angelin Jones Simmons. In the service of the gospel, each has taken seriously my vocational call to proclaim "Thus saith the Lord."

Introduction

R EAD, IF YOU WILL, THIS BOOK as if each lecture is a definitive line drawn in the sand differentiating between jackleg preachers and professionals of the Word of God. Its overall idea forms a gargantuan divide. On one side of the chasm are fraudulent impostors who prostitute the Christian gospel as unscrupulous charlatans; on the other side are Christian ministers who embody preaching as holy intellectual inquiry.

In addition, these chapters may be a refresher course for hundreds of seminarians who studied with Isaac Rufus Clark, Sr., during his twenty-seven year tenure (1962–1989) as Fuller E. Callaway Professor of Homiletics at the Interdenominational Theological Center in Atlanta, Georgia. Clark, who loved teaching preaching, is curiously absent (but in name only) from the dozens of sermon anthologies and the handful of publications on black homiletics; yet to those of us familiar with his life's work, the traces of Clark's remarkable influence on contemporary preaching are identifiable in black pulpit activities throughout this nation, the Caribbean, and in several countries in Africa.

As one of the most serious and demanding preaching professors of the twentieth century, Clark advances a clear mandate that the work of homiletics and the explication of sermon delivery require the complex development of a theoethical consciousness. Specialized devices of oratory, diction, and modes of argumentation should never take center stage in sermon preparation. Instead, Clark directs his critical attention to the acknowledgment of theological education as the underpinning for bona fide preachers. Those who studied with him will remember how Clark challenged prevailing unquestioning, homegrown assumptions of black communities:

There is no such animal in all creation as a holy person who is ignorant about holy things. There is no such monkey under God's
heaven as a holy monkey who has a vacuum of understanding about
holy things in God's world. There is no such animal as a holy
preacher without the benefit of deep, holy knowledge about holy
things gained somewhere in somebody's holy school. Ain't no use in
putting out that damnable lie about being a holy preacher without
first having sat under a holy-person-of-God-in-the-know in somebody's holy school.

Then again, this book may be needed as a distinct, clearly accessible homiletical practicum for ministers today who were trained
in other theological institutions and were taught by other preaching professors. After years of pulpit experience they struggle from
Sunday to Sunday to find their ethical voices in the preparation of
each and every sermon. In lucid and forceful language, Clark
extends a sharp polemical invitation to participate in his preaching
course in this way:

> No dumb homiletical monkey can preach a holy sermon no kind of
> way. I don't care how many benches you tipped over in your
> funkmaking days. If you ain't sat under a person-in-the-know who
> can teach you about the deeper things of preaching under God, then
> you haven't done nothing but participate in a funkmaking show.

This book is Clark's master guide, the result of many years of study
and reflection on nearly every aspect of preaching in the black
church community.

The opportunity to translate the profound prophetic truth, "If
you ain't got no proposition, you ain't got no sermon neither!"
which serves as the core thesis in the work of Isaac R. Clark, Sr., is
a cause for celebration. A lifelong member of the African
Methodist Episcopal Church, Clark (February 25, 1925–January 18,
1990) was the fourth child of the Reverend James H. and Lillian
Clark of New Castle, Pennsylvania. After graduating from the
New Castle public schools in 1943, Clark served honorably in the
United States Navy until 1946. He received the Bachelor of Arts
degree from Wilberforce University in 1951 and his Bachelor of
Divinity degree from Payne Theological Seminary in 1952, the
year he was ordained an elder. He was awarded the Doctor of The-

ology degree in systematic theology in 1958 from Boston University, after successfully defending his dissertation, "Redemption in the Thought of Albert Knudson and Emil Brunner." As his career developed, Clark served pastorates in Milford, Ohio, and in Lynn and New Bedford, Massachusetts. Prior to joining the faculty at the Interdenominational Theological Center (ITC) in 1962, he taught systematic theology at Payne Theological Seminary in Wilberforce, Ohio, and religion and philosophy at Paul Quinn College in Waco, Texas.

I count myself as one among hundreds of Isaac R. Clark's preaching protégés, but I was the one singled out by Clark to make sure that his distinct homiletical methodology received the critical attention it deserves in the twenty-first century. My explicit intent is clearly presentational. This book brings Clark face-to-face with a reading audience, allowing him to explain the formal elements of preaching from the inside out. Each chapter, or lecture, mediates its own message.

James H. Costen, the former president of ITC, appropriately articulates the serious import of Clark's distinct commitment to the academic teaching of black homiletics:

> Almost as one singly commissioned by God to look out for God's people, Clark waged a one person war against all those students and others who took a cavalier, uncaring and sloppy attitude toward their preaching or other forms of communication. His forte was clear, precise, cogent, organized and prophetic utterance. Other than this was an abomination. He felt so deeply on this subject because of his deep love for the Saints, the beloved people of God. Therefore, a sermon for him needed to be an offering acceptable to God, no less acceptable than the most adequate gift of our time, our energy, our imagination, and our financial resources.[1]

In undertaking this task I have conceived of my responsibility as that of making more readily available the gold mine of Clark's instructions regarding the nature of rhetorical strategies and their

---

[1] James H. Costen, Sr., "Reflections upon the Life of I. R. Clark," for the Consultation on Black Preaching, November 14–16, 1990, at the Interdenominational Theological Center in Atlanta, Georgia.

underlying ethics in establishing the preaching stage as a sending forth place in the work of justice.

Clark's battle cry, "If you ain't got no proposition, you ain't got no sermon neither!" signals a task much more substantial than chastising seminarians from buying into "cheap solutions for things that require long-term, internal resolutions." The proposition is the central, integrating, controlling sentence of the entire sermonic discourse, embracing in its makeup a clear, procedural *how*-meaning that is added to an already established and previously given *what*-meaning (Title/Subject) and *why*-meaning (Introduction) of the discourse—in essence by means of that one, central, integrating, controlling sentence of the sermon. The proposition grabs the title/subject and the essence of the introduction in order to harness these meanings to the body of the sermon.

The proposition lets the hearers know where they are going, so they will never be sermonically "lost." Being spiritually lost is the devil's doing; being sermonically lost is the preacher's doing! Sermons are not mazes or mysteries. The proposition lets the preacher know what s/he is about as s/he brings material to the sermon for construction. The proposition, like the title/subject, should be like a plumb line for judging genuine or spurious material. "If you ain't got no proposition, you ain't got no sermon neither!"

Each part of Clark's homiletical process—the text, title, introduction, proposition, body points, and conclusion—forces the preaching student to engage the conceptual space that embraces the theoretical construction of preaching as an incarnational, "emmanuel" experience, "God is here with us." Such a claim might seem hyperbolic were it not for the fact that Clark's delineated, detailed lectures bear witness to such possibilities.

By means of a literal, etymological definition of the term itself, Clark tells us that homiletics is composed of the elision of two words, namely, *homily* and *rhetoric*. Employing this notion, Clark explains that an elision is where two words are intermixed to form one word and some of the letters in the original words drop out in a new combined word. Thus, *homiletics* is the deliberate syllable-reducing consonantalization of *homily* and *rhetoric*.

In a fuller, more theological explanation, Clark illustrates the dynamic hybridity that is fundamental to homiletics. *Homily,* derived from Greek, is related to the root word *homoios*, meaning one and the same, familiar kind. For example, we have the term *homo sapiens*, meaning those humans who have the same, familiar kind of learning capacities as over against other creatures; *homo*-sexual, meaning the same, familiar kind of sexual orientation, interests, and desires; *homo*-genized milk, meaning that the milk is the same, familiar kind throughout the bottle; *home*, meaning all who share the same, familiar kind of family rules in the same household.

> Again, for example, the same, familiar kind of reality that held the Israelites together was the experience of being delivered from bondage by the same God of Abraham, Sarah and Hagar. So the homily of the biblical prophets was made in the name of Jehovah, the same, familiar God of the wandering, nomadic people who the Lord brought up out of slavery, out of the house of bondage. And likewise, the homily of Christians is that God was in Christ reconciling the world, so we, as Christians, can say that Jesus is our home-boy because Jesus is the same, familiar kind of reality to and for us Christians.

Next Clark concerns himself with defining *rhetoric*, another Greek term, the second half of the word *homiletics*. Rhetoric is the art of attaching speech to effective logic in persuading, convincing, and edifying the judgment of one's hearers.[2] It means presenting logical evidence using the various techniques of argumentation, in order for preachers to bring to the mind of hearers the "presence" of matters that are of ultimate concern. In other words, rhetoric has to do with understanding how women and men think in order to know what it takes to convince them to buy what we are selling.[3]

---

[2] For descriptive foundational texts on rhetoric, see Aristotle, *Rhetoric and Poetics*, trans. W. Rhys (Oxford: Modern Library, 1924); Amos Wilder, *Early Christian Rhetoric: The Language of the Gospel* (London: SCM, 1964; rpt., Cambridge, Mass.: Harvard University Press, 1971); and George A. Kennedy, *Classical Rhetoric and Its Christian and Secular Tradition: From Ancient to Modern Times* (Chapel Hill: University of North Carolina Press, 1980).

[3] On the evolution of African American rhetorical forms, see Alice Moore Dunbar, ed., *Masterpieces of Negro Eloquence* (New York: Bookery Publish-

And whether we know it or not, our task as Professional Proclaimers is to make sales for God concerning Jesus Christ, our homeboy. So, when we add this rhetorical concern to the homily concern, we come up with the term homiletics, which means to express the meaning of the Gospel in a way that women, men, and children can buy it for their living.

According to Clark's pedagogical objective, the essence of black preaching, as it has developed from the antebellum era to the present, can be summarized in five stages: (1) *divine activity,* wherein (2) the *Word of God* is (3) *proclaimed* or *announced* (4) on a *contemporary issue* (5) with an *ultimate response* to our God.

Clark's comprehensive five-part definition of preaching is—in the way of all good rhetoric—about the creation of effective oral communication. Like the spirituals, Clark's work provides us with theoethical negotiations and liberating strategies for talking to the human soul; and also like the spirituals, his lectures insist that genuine proclaimers of divine truth can be free of all traces of "jack-leggism," if we orient ourselves to the holiness of this sacred task.

We all need to be perfectly clear about the holy objectives in this course, so that no ignorant fool will think fallaciously that we are trying to produce jacklegs for the pulpit. There are too many jack-legs climbing up into too many pulpits now. And we are not interested in turning loose no more of that kind of garbage on the people.

Jackleg preachers need to be carried to a toilet and flushed down the drain in a sewer somewhere, away from the affairs of people on earth. The determination of whether a person is a jackleg has to do with the content of one's character, whether or not such rascals have sided with the devil at the core of their being.

Some readers will find Clark's indicative style overpowering. For instance, in a gesture of radical transformation, Clark makes

---

ing, 1914); Carter G. Woodson, *Negro Orators and Their Orations* (Washington, D.C.: Associated Pub., 1925); Marcus H. Boulware, *The Oratory of Negro Leaders, 1900–1968* (Westport, Conn.: Negro University Press, 1969); Bettye Collier Thomas, *Daughters of Thunder: Black Women Preachers and Their Sermons, 1850–1979* (San Francisco: Jossey-Bass, 1997); Dolan Hubbard, *The Sermon and the African American Literary Imagination* (Columbia: University of Missouri Press, 1994); Cleophus J. LaRue, *The Heart of Black Preaching* (Louisville: Westminster John Knox, 2000).

explicit his objective in the initial meeting of the year-long preaching course. With humor and righteous indignation, Clark resorts to all kinds of creative examples and homegrown analogies, so that students grasp that the issue at stake is the dialectic and dialogic tension between the personal matter—the preacher—and the subject matter—the preaching. This tension is necessarily constant, with the personal matter being uppermost.

Dramatizing the impetus for this first leg of the homiletical journey, dealing with basic understandings of messenger and message, Clark presents the voice of a seminarian who objects wholeheartedly to his thesis.

> Well now, Doc done got besides himself, talking about you can't be no holy preacher without some training under a person-of-God-in-the-know in somebody's holy school first. Well, let me tell you something. I don't go for that, because I have preached some powerful sermons long before I heard tell of a seminary. I have had the folks turn church out with my preaching, long before I enrolled here. Doc, you are wrong! I know from experience that what you are saying is not so!
>
> And furthermore, Doc needs to be informed that Jesus was a very holy preacher and Jesus never had any training in anybody's holy school. I am looking ever unto Jesus for my source of power, regardless of what Doc is saying about training in somebody's holy school, and about being under some holy-person-of-God-in-the-know. Jesus!

Clark responds by avowing once again that the relation between the preacher and the sermon is primary and of utmost importance.

> The damnable lie about Jesus not having no training in somebody's holy school always comes up every year at this time. And, when unholy jackasses tell that damn lie on our Lord Jesus, they need to be cussed out with some holy four-letter words. And in addition, they need to have their asses kicked. Turn the whole class loose, so as to hold them and to kick their asses for telling that damn lie on the Lord Jesus in an unholy way like that. I would rather hear less about preaching and pray all day long, than to hear a monkey tell a damn lie like that on the Lord Jesus.

In this declaration Clark emphasizes the non-negotiable, underlying principle of the integration of person and subject in order to avoid the pitfall of the division of end and means in the development and delivery of the sermon. Too often the historical Jesus is not the point of departure in a preaching course. Because of the very nature of homily and rhetoric, discussions of the Jesus of history as a preacher may occur in Bible and theology classes but not necessarily as the entry point in homiletics. In contrast, Clark situates the image of Jesus as student teacher as the site for preaching in his course. Obviously influenced by the liberating traditions of the black church and his conscious, self-reflexive process as a systematic theologian, Clark is deeply concerned with providing seminarians with a transformative vision that focuses on Jesus as the chief cornerstone of our preaching person as well as of our preaching subject.

> That is why we must learn about Jesus' solid background in education in somebody's holy school. Everybody knows that Jesus took a chance on getting a whipping by being left behind in Jerusalem at the age of twelve in order to sit at the feet of those doctors and lawyers in the temple. I am not denying that Jesus was answering questions, but he was also getting answers to the questions that he raised with the doctors and lawyers about the height and depth of theology. If Jesus had been spending all of his time with jacklegs, then they would not have been able to answer his questions. And, that is why Jesus took a chance on getting a whipping when he ran into a pot of theological gold in the temple in Jerusalem.

Continuing to elaborate his response to the question about Jesus' theological education, Clark in a remarkably pedagogic way points students to biblical narratives (based on John 1) and the church's kergyma, which bring Jesus and John the Baptist together in the earthly career of Jesus. Clark introduces into the argument the idea that the two men were closely associated for a time.

> Everyone knows that Jesus was taught by and graduated summa cum laude at the school of John the Baptist, the holy-man-of-God-in-the-know. Jesus was baptized in the Jordan by John and sent out with his Master of Divinity degree having been taught theology and homiletics by John the Baptist. That is why Jesus' message and John the Baptist's message were the same. John the Baptist was preaching in the wilderness, REPENT, for the kingdom of heaven is at hand. And, when Jesus came out of the wilderness, he said the same thing, REPENT, for the kingdom of heaven is at hand. Now where did Jesus

get that message, that theology? From John the Baptist, his old teacher, that man-of-God-in-the-know.

Optimistically, Clark moves his argument to a deeper plane. Unlike the popular false teaching concerning Jesus' lack of theological education, Clark believes that Jesus said, "There is none better under God's heaven than John the Baptist, my former teacher, that man-of-God-in-the-know, who taught me theology and homiletics." John the Baptist also said, according to Clark, "There is none better than Jesus, whom I greatly revere. Jesus is the greatest student I ever had. I didn't put anything out that Jesus couldn't learn. Jesus was an A+, a summa cum laude person. Yes siree! I know because I taught him." In this dramatization, Clark is concerned with rectifying the warped, distorted lie wherein holy character is disconnected from theological education.

For many first-year preaching students, this argument evokes disturbing memories of their own mis-education about Jesus from their formative years in church school as well as the countless hours in the eleven o'clock worship service. Even though the necessary factual materials (places, dates, events, sequences) are not available to write the complete story of Jesus' theological education, Clark maintains that it would be a damnable lie if such skepticism or literalism were to lead to a complete dismissal of interest in the earthly Jesus' preparation for ministry. The question of what can be known about Jesus' training in theological preaching is an extraordinarily difficult one—but that does not mean that no attempt should be made to answer it.

In contrast to preaching professors who primarily teach theatrical techniques and use tentative language in public speaking—I suspect, I hope, I guess, I reckon, I suppose—separating faith convictions of the messenger from the message, the end product from the embodied means, Clark insists that there is a living divine connection between the preacher and the proclamation. This inextricable relation between preacher and proclamation must never be broken without transgressing the will of God. Thus, Clark's cultivation of a self-conscious indicative mode for proclaiming the Word of God is based on the moral necessity of gaining deep insights into the nature and purpose of the subject matter in order to be well off in the personal matter.

Again, others may ask, "Why is Clark so adamant that a test for the true and sincere preacher requires that we know the signs of God if we are going to be able to hear God talking to us, if we are going to obey God spiritually?" Fundamental to this discourse on *homiletics as holy intellectual inquiry* is Clark's central understanding that God gives us physical instructors to teach us to hear God speaking in the physical world. Nature is the only way that we can pick up on the voice of God Almighty. The relevance of Clark's interesting and informative viewpoint is that he shows how and why ethical character and physical things are integral to each other.

Within the parameters of exemplification, Clark uses various biblical records to construct his argument, such stories as that of Hagar hearing the angel of the Lord calling from heaven as she wanders and weeps in the wilderness of Beersheba and her eyes being opened so that she sees the well of water in her midst; Moses in the Midian desert where the bush burns but is not consumed; Elijah experiencing the sound of silence in the darkened cave while in flight as a fugitive; and the peal of thunder from the heavens with a dove descending to light on Jesus' shoulder at his baptism in the Jordan River. Something physical is needed in order for us to be aware of the presence of God. In consequence, Clark says,

> Ain't no possible way to have a legitimate divine human encounter without some physical instrument making that divine encounter possible. There is always some physical instrumentality involved in every legitimate encounter with the living God and the entire critical record proves it.
>
> So ain't no need of you talking about you are going to be a preacher and don't know the signs, because it means that you can't hear God talking to you if you don't know God's physical world.

The Bible's testimony to the connection between morality and physical instrumentality is evident in every legitimate encounter with the living God. Even the original disciples, Clark argues, heard sounds such as the rushing of a mighty wind in the upper room at Pentecost, a physical manifestation accompanying the visitation of the Holy Spirit. God speaks to us through such physical mediation all the time. Clark is talking specifically about theophanic invitations as the theology of divine presence.

God knows our physical frame. That is why God created a physical world long before God created human beings. God knew that there needed to be physical instruments through which to communicate with us. And thus, God's heavens are telling the divine story to us and the firmament is showing forth God's handiwork. Loving God with all our heart means that we make it our divine business to learn about God's physical world so that we can know better how to listen to the voice of God when God speaks to us through mediative physicality.

That is why I still say that there is no such animal as a holy preacher without the benefit of deep, holy knowledge about holy things ordained in somebody's holy school under a person-of-God-in-the-know. God knows our physical frame, even as preachers. That is why God gives us physical homiletics teachers so that we can be led to hear more clearly the voice of God speaking to us on the deeper meanings and implications of the things of homiletics in proclaiming God's holy word.

Still, a few may become spellbound by Clark's colorfully adorned vocabulary, even mesmerized by his descriptive metaphors and the drama of his expressive vernacular of double negatives. Some may be turned off by the stinging sharpness of his speech. Clark's verbal nouns, signifying wordplay, deliberate redundancy, and colloquially coined cussedness that permeate these lectures may cause one or two readers to miss Clark's keen analyses and profound complexities. As Clark points out, the language in each of his lectures makes possible and welcomes exchange between the students and the professor in conjunction with a daily prayer for the Holy Spirit to be active in the presentation of the subject matter. Clark says that he wants to use the most communicative kind of human expressions for convincing and persuading men and women to live creatively under God, which is crucial in expressing faith meaningfully for edifying the saints and for winning unbelievers to our God. In essence, Clark's language is grounded in a non-negotiable theological mandate: to apply the principles of rhetoric to the particular ends and means of the Christian gospel, for the purpose of liberation, reconciliation, and maturation in the deepest theological sense of the term, so that as professionals of the Word of God we will never be guilty of unconsciously tampering with people's souls.

The challenge of this work, as I see it, is to open up a broader discussion of Clark's scholarship for generations who are unacquainted with his seminal efforts, as well as to provide evidence for assisting colleagues in drawing their own conclusions in the evaluation of my claim of Clark's homiletical genius. Clark's is not the only methodology that emerged in my research on Christian ethics in the academic teaching of homiletics, but it is one of the strongest of those time-tested, black touchstones for determining the quality of genuineness in the African American pulpit.[4]

---

[4] Preaching as developed among African Americans has had a long and significant history. It is important to note those who analyzed oral sacred rhetoric for the purpose of critical homiletical construction. See Henry H. Mitchell, *Black Preaching* (Philadelphia: J. B. Lippincott, 1970); Mervyn A. Warren, *Black Preaching: Truth and Soul* (Washington, D.C.: University Press of America, 1977); Lawrence Beale, *Toward a Black Homiletics* (New York: Vantage, 1978); J. Alfred Smith, Sr., *Preach On! A Concise Handbook of the Element of Style in Preaching* (Nashville: Broadman, 1984); Warren Stewart, *Interpreting God's Word in Black Preaching* (Valley Forge, Pa.: Judson Press, 1984); James Forbes, *The Holy Spirit and Preaching* (Nashville: Abingdon, 1989); Samuel D. Proctor and Gardner C. Taylor, *The Certain Sound of the Trumpet: Crafting a Sermon of Authority* (Valley Forge, Pa.: Judson Press, 1994); Amos Jones, *As You Go Preach: Dynamics of Sermon Building and Preaching in the Black Church* (Nashville: Bethlehem Book Pub., 1997); Brian K. Blount, *Go Preach! Mark's Kingdom Message and the Black Church Today* (Maryknoll, N.Y.: Orbis Books, 1998); and Samuel K. Roberts, ed., *Born to Preach: Essays in Honor of the Ministry of Henry and Ella Mitchell* (Valley Forge, Pa.: Judson Press, 2000).

1

Taking the Holiness of Preaching Seriously

Proposition: *Therefore, if an understanding of holy things abides in this course, and if the life of our Lord proves that Jesus' holy character was nourished by his deep understanding of holy things, and if we ourselves are determined to be more than conquerors in Jesus' name, then let us make it our business to learn about the deep things of this holy course in two significant ways.*

THE PROPOSITION STATED ABOVE testifies to two deep convictions about the holy principles in this homiletics course. In the first place, you must grasp a radical understanding regarding the theological character of the historical Jesus, who was nourished by his knowledge of holy things. The other significant concern is that if you are going to be more than conquerors in the name of Jesus, you must look not only at what is *written on* the course contract, but you must *go behind* the syllabus so that you understand the unseen principles and ideas in the makeup of our holy homiletics course. This latter concern refers to the effort of the maker, what the creator of this holy course had in mind when he created this *holy intellectual inquiry*. The things that we see are made by things that we do not see.

In view of these twofold convictions, a basic idea that brings this holy course into being is that I intend it from its very beginning to be holy. And because the holy intention is such a deep conviction in my original thought, I have no reservations about referring to this course with the adjective *holy*. And hear this, "it is indeed holy in fact!"

Well now, Doc done got beside himself again. Doc certainly can't mean that this course is holy. What does Doc mean by calling this course, of all courses, holy? If it is so holy, as Doc claims, then where is the altar? And the candles? And the burning incense? And the Holy Bible? Doc ain't never brought no Bible here, but one day. Seems like we would have some holy things around this place if this course is really holy, like Doc just said. In fact, Doc ain't even had no prayer since the first day. So how in the devil can a thing be holy without the power of prayer?

And too, it seems kind of unholy to me with all that nasty talk that Doc puts out every day. All the time, every day talking about monkeys and jacklegs and jackasses and rumps and butts and buncom-buncoms. Seldom does Doc even mention the precious name of Jesus. Doc has been carrying on something terrible with his filthy-talking mouth. And now, all of a sudden, Doc is trying to be sanctimonious and pious after carrying on all the devilment thus far, talking about theological character and ethical integrity with his lying self. And talking about holiness with his unholy, filthy-talking self. Doc ain't nothin' but a liar and thief. Doc needs to be converted himself before he can talk about anything holy.

We need to get that unholy monkey to the mourner's bench for a long season of prayer. Doc needs to be born again himself. Doc needs to be born again before he tries to teach us another day about proclaiming God's holy word. And we need to bring a brick to throw it at his unholy self.

Maybe there is some truth in all the indictments. Maybe this is something that I need to think about. And maybe I desperately need to be born again, because all of us need lots of help, and I in particular have not made my approach to that highest prize yet. I need to think carefully about this student's indictment against me. "So take me to the water, take me to the water, take me to the water to be baptized. Take us to the water, take us to the water, take us to the water to be baptized."

And if you want to take me down for a long season of prayer, I'll buy that too. I desperately need a whole lot of help in regard to things holy. So take me to the water and to the mourner's bench for some prayer, if you think that will help me. But before you take me to the water and begin that long season of prayer with me, let me clarify why I still have no reservation calling this homiletics course *holy*. I still have no scruples about calling this course *holy* in spite of my vulgar language, and in spite of my lack of prayer in this class.

So maybe, just maybe, oftentimes it might be me, but maybe, you are the one who is unholy. Maybe, just maybe, you need to think about that too. I have good reason for calling this course that I created *holy*. And you need to hear those good reasons with your dumb, shallow, silly idiotic self, before you try to haul someone else's buncom-buncom to the altar for a long season of prayer.

First of all, let me inform you, fool, whence I am speaking when I use the term *holy* in reference to this course. I am not using the term *holy* in the same sense as the average monkey on the street and in some churches. I ain't gettin' the meaning of the term *holy* from dumb monkeys in the street. The meaning of *holy* in this course comes from a little book by an eminent scholar, Rudolph Otto. Otto's classical book in the Christian tradition is *The Idea of the Holy*.

I dare to say that the author Rudolph Otto does not have a black butt, and yet, I cannot see how anybody can be blackenized in their souls without capturing the deep belief and the critical significance of Otto's *Idea of the Holy*. I suspect that is the reason why so many theologians make this book required reading in their courses. I would dare further to say that if one does not capture the deep meaning and significance of the *holy* in the sense that Rudolph Otto is writing, then you have no business fumbling around up there on that preaching stage, trying to lead anybody in a divine worship service, ever.

Without a deep understanding of the meaning of the *holy* in Otto's sense, then you ain't doin' nothin' but spreading an unholy epidemic on a gang of idiots trying to participate in that so-called holy worship service. Even when the preacher's robe is a'swishin' every which-a-way, and the organ is bathing our souls in a melodious rendition of "Sweet Hour of Prayer," and some members are jumping like monkeys until the place get funky, still it is nothing more than spreading an unholy epidemic on a gang of idiots by an idiot with a nasty collar on backwards, if the meaning of *holy* as Rudolph Otto defines it is not behind that religious carnival. It is funkmaking, just plain funkmaking.

Funkmaking and being unholy are the same identical thing. It doesn't matter who makes the funk, and in what church, and when and where the funk is being made. And it makes no difference how many fools say that they enjoy it every Sunday. If it is not in line with what Rudolph Otto is saying, then it is still ignorant, unholy funkmaking for nobody but the devil and his crowd.

Well now, what does Rudolph Otto mean by the term *holy*? What is the deeper meaning and significance of *The Idea of the Holy*? What Otto means primarily is that the idea of the *holy* has to do with something distinctive in quality of being. *Holy* means something unique, something with a character that is different from the common world of things in existence. *Holy* means something that nothing else is like in kind, no where. And it is in light of this distinctive, unique, particular, different meaning of *holy* that Rudolph Otto endeavors to think and talk about God.

God, accordingly, to Otto, must be thought about and talked about as being absolutely distinctive in kind of being as the Creator over against all other creatures, for there is none like God in existence. Nowhere, says Rudolph Otto.

Well now, let's see if we can apply this just a little bit to this preaching course. If *The Idea of the Holy* has special reference to the character and being of God as over against all other creatures, then what does all that have to do with this course being *holy*? That is the big relevant question that emerges on this scene. When we say that *holy* refers to God, then how can we also say that *holy* refers to this course?

Let me begin this application of the meaning of *holy* to this course by assuring you that what we do *with* and *for* and *on* and *to* you will be different from what is done in any other course at this seminary. This preaching course is different-in-kind. And it may be different from anything that will ever be done to you in this world. This preaching course is distinctive, unique, different-in-kind in terms of what will be done *with*, *to*, and *for* you, and *holy* in the distinctive way that it will work *on* you.

Thus, you can be sure, you can be very sure, that we will not be dealing with preaching relevant meals in unholy ways. It will not be business as usual in our consideration of preaching like everybody else does. We ain't goin' to be teaching what the average, unholy jackleg says and thinks about preaching. Don't even look for it in this course.

We deliberately intend to put something on you and do something to you that ain't never been done before, no where. And we deliberately hope that it will be so *holy*, so different, so unique, so different-in-kind that you ain't never goin' to forget it, either. This course is *holy* is terms of your remembering what happened to you in this class, remembering in that unique sense, for as long as you live.

Furthermore, this course will be real *holy* in another peculiar sense, because the monkey running this show, and who made up the contract for it, is indeed different from every other monkey at this school, and in the world, for that matter. And don't you ever forget it. And don't try to treat me like you treat everybody else. I is who I is! There is no one else in existence like me, and that makes all the difference in the world. The kind of monkey running the show makes a big difference in the way the drama is played.

So you need to understand as much as you can about the mind of the creator of that holy course proposition. Otherwise you will be bumping into a lot of things throughout the course that will not make the deepest kind of sense to you. Thus, you do need to understand what this peculiar homiletics professor has in his crazy mind, invisibly *behind* the makeup of this holy course's contract, and then you will understand better what is *on* it.

And for a more personal, private matter, this course will also be *holy* in still another real sense—namely, in terms of its peculiar design with you in mind as its ultimate *holy* objective. We do deliberately intend for you to be a distinctive, unique, and different-in-kind preacher as a result of having been here. We do expect for you to become really different preachers, as a consequence of having been in this course. *Holy* in an expected-preacher sense is our ultimate objective with you in mind also.

And make no mistake about it. You had better be clear in your mind before the time of dropping courses is over because you ain't goin' to be like you were, if you stay in this course. Thus, I order you this day, to put off thy shoes in reverence and respect for things *holy* about this place. Get thy shoes off and keep them off as long as you are around these *holy* premises. In fact, be sure to take your shoes off even before you enter this *holy* room every day. You need to get *holy* before you come in here so that you can be in this *holy* room with reverence and respect for *holy* things around this place every day. This is indeed *holy* ground with a *holy* purpose for your *holy* preaching character for the rest of your *holy* preaching life. You need to know that. And you need to be acting like you know that every time you come in here in God's *holy* name. You need to look like and act like this is indeed *holy* ground in this room every day, *holy* in that peculiar looking and acting sense.

Thus, one indivisible idea in my mind in the divine makeup of this course is the idea of homiletics being *holy* in every respect. Holy! Holy! Holy! Lord God Almighty! Real holy! Something distinctive, unique, and different-in-kind to make a divine difference in the affairs of people under the banner of our heavenly, holy Father who called us into this holy preaching business in the name of Our Lord. Amen! And Amen!

2

Bearing the Cross
in This Holy Course

Bearing the Cross deals with our willingness to shed blood, sweat, and tears for the removal of our preaching sins, in terms of being made aware of the divine and human dimensions in the study of homiletics, so that we are able to see what we need to master through informational familiarity, if we want to enhance our God-given talents as a power base for proclaiming out of the depths of our existence, authentically.

TODAY WE MOVE ON TO DISCUSS what is written *on* that holy contract. Wasn't that the proposition? That we will look *behind* the contract and then we will look *on* it, which is the second order of our holy proposition for understanding the principles of this holy course. So, let us begin by finding out the rest of that propositional mandate by wrestling with the question *why* as related to the objective of our homiletics course.

Concluding *behind* the scenes from our previous lecture, in order for you to understand the invisible reality that produced the holy proposition, it should be obvious by now, I have nothing in mind for you but a cross. If you have gotten the full impact of *The Idea of the Holy*, then that discussion should have made it perfectly clear that I have nothing in mind for you but some kind of double-cross.

Now here I am talking about a cross for you and I ain't mentioned nothing about the resurrection for you. I am talking about a cross or, more accurately, some kind of double-cross for you. Thus, with all that kind of nasty, crazy talk about your buncom hanging on a cross, one serious haunting question must be in the center of your mind by now. Maybe that serious haunting question is *WHY*?

Why all that silly, stupid, downright crazy talk about crucifying our buncoms in this course, Doc? *Why* is there an intentional whipping for us in this course, Doc? *Why?* That kind of serious haunting question must be emerging in the center of your minds by now or long before, unless you are just plain dumb. *Why,* Doc? *Why* must it be all the day long?

And just because I was aware of the inevitability of the question *why,* I have deliberately set aside some time to get to the basic *why* of this course, relevant to its cross-bearing nature. And in passing let me say that there are three kinds of questions that are always raised in any meaningful dialogue, including even in our preaching dialogue.

Preaching is dialogue. That doesn't mean that the parishioners are actually running their mouths back at you, but it does mean that as you talk, questions emerge. If you have any sense, then you answer the questions in your listeners' minds. Always dialogue. Every time you say one sentence, there is a question of some kind that is raised, so you begin to respond to that question. Otherwise, you ain't preaching—if you are not answering the needs of the folk for whom you are raising these questions in their minds.

Now, these three basic questions of meaning are some form of the questions *what, how,* and *why.* I am going to give you a little test, and I want you to tell me which question is raised in your mind by certain statements I will make to you.

Suppose I said that a man is giving out fifty-dollar bills to all persons who can prove that they attend this seminary. What question would you raise? *Where?* You are right. You don't ask *why* the man is giving them out; you are going to ask *where* is he? Where is that man?

Suppose I said this to you: the best thing for you to do in order to become a really effective preacher is to sit your buncom on a red-hot stove for about two seconds before you try to preach. *Why?* Yes, if you have a difficult thing to do, then you will want to know *why.* Just like when we tell folks, "YOU KNOW YOU OUGHT TO BEAR YOUR CROSS!" They don't want to know *how* to do that; they are going to want to know *why.* You got to prove that bearing your cross will produce some fruit for them. No one is going to get up there on that cross, if you haven't told them why they need to do it. What we are saying is that every statement we make, in or out of the pulpit, should relate to answering one of those three basic questions of meaning.

Well now, what then is the meaning of this most profound *why* that always emerges when we face difficult situations? What is it about this question that makes you say *why* when I say that you ought to sit on a hot stove for about two seconds? What does *why* mean by definition?

Generally speaking, we can say that this most profound question has to do with probing the basic cause or intention or reason or purpose for the existence of something or someone, so as to get to the basic gut meaning of that something or someone. It is the foundational probing question by which we have identified what is there confronting us for a meaningful relationship. We know *what* it is. It is a cross. That is something that we know anywhere. Just because it is there and we understand that it is there, we then ponder about its basic cause or intention or reason or purpose for being there for meaningful relationship—the *why* of it being there.

You know that there is a cross in this homiletics course. You can identify that. Confronting us is the issue of *why* is a cross here. What is the meaning in the cross being here? *Why* is that profound question for getting at a basic understanding of anything in existence. And you know, and I know, and God Almighty knows, that whatever can aid us in basic understanding has got to be the biggest and the mostest in the kingdom of God. Because we said in the beginning that understanding is the chief thing to seek after in any creative endeavor. When we understand *why*, it feeds us all the day long. Then and only then can we cheer up and live creatively in the sunshine of life. Wanting the meaning of the *why* question makes it possible to live with some meaning and cheer in our existence.

Was not, for instance, this most profound question the secret behind Job's dilemma? It was not so much the agony, pain, and frustration that Job endured from a physical point of view, though we should not minimize that physical frustration, because physical pain and disease are not light matters for humans to deal with. But the deepest frustration of Job's suffering had to do with the unresolved reason for his terrible agony. If he could only find out the *why* of his suffering, Job was sure that he could cheer up and live creatively in the sunshine of life and accept it gladly and willingly. But Job could not discover the reason for his tragic dilemma. Everybody, including Job, knew that Job was a holy, God-fearing man and did not deserve such tragedy in his human affairs. And that is why Job wanted to have an encounter with the Almighty. I want to find God so that I might plead my case. *Why* have you done me this injustice? I have been a good father and a good husband. And there are people around here robbing and shooting and killing and I ain't been doing that and they are walking around in good health. *Why* me? *Why* was the essence of Job's soul-searching dilemma on his bed of affliction ages ago.

Again, for example, the same question is the first issue raised by Our Lord in his agony on the cross. He didn't ask *What* is this? Or *How* is this? But, my God, my God, *why?* *Why* have you allowed this to happen to me in whom you declared publicly that you found special delight in the affairs of humankind? For what cause, what intention, for what reason, for what purpose is this happening to me, your only-begotten son? *Why* is the very essence of Jesus' dilemma at Calvary and the first question he raised at Calvary, *"My God, My God, why has thy forsaken me?"* And in finding a meaningful, theological resolution to that big *why* dilemma Our Lord concludes with confidence, while still in agony on the cross, saying this, "I see now that my divine work on earth is really finished." There is no reason for me to continue in existence any longer. There is cause for me to go out in a dramatic way so that the world will never forget what happened this day and what I meant to the world."

And when you have done your work there is no need to keep hanging around. You need to be in a grave somewhere because you have no reason for living any more, unless you have a purpose that you are working on. So, into thy hands do I confidently commend my spirit. Why could Jesus say that? All because he had found the answer to that most profound question he raised in agony on the cross. *Why* Lord? was the question in Jesus' soul-shaking dilemma. Jesus became liberated when he found the answer to that *why* dilemma deep down in his soul on the cross that day.

And still again for example, the same profound *why* is the most inevitable question that a child continuously raises as it clings to its mother's knee seeking the deep meaning of its new-found life. *Why*, Mommy, *why* is the continuous soul-disturbing question, all day long. And that is a hard question to answer. *What* is easy to answer sometimes. And *how* is easy to answer if you have a grip on the handle. But *why* it should be thus? *Why* Mommy? Ain't no easy question to answer.

And this same group of profound *why* questions is still on the lips of every person we meet. Even crazy people with one foot in the grave are still just as baffled by the riddle of this big *why* question as a young child at his mother's knee. Some people have not found the deep meaning of that question in their lives, not one day. Few people, very few people, ever solve the riddle about the deepest meaning of their lives. They live their whole lives and do not get one iota about *why* they have lived under God's heaven. And because few people ever find the answer to that *why* question, that comprehensive question has profound meaning for most of us and is the riddle of our existence. Which says, tell me why. TELL ME WHY!

And so for this cause, for this reason, for this purpose, we lay before you our overall objective, giving you the necessary *why* of it in the deepest understanding of the cross-bearing nature of this course. You have stumbled into Jerusalem in coming here. And we do have a heavy cross for you to bear. We have a cross just waiting for you to pick it up, and then to carry it up a hill, and then to hop your buncom on it, and then permit yourself to be nailed to it, voluntarily. Just because we expect that of you, voluntarily, we are sure that you need some deep, reasonable answers concerning *why* it must be thus, all the day long in this holy enterprise.

So let us begin to roll back some of those billowing clouds over your souls by wrestling with that overall objective in our holy contract so that we can make a stab at the deepest kind of meaning in this holy enterprise. It is in such wrestling that we just might come up with the basic cause or intention or reason or purpose as to *why* it must be thus all the day long in this cross-bearing course. And maybe, just maybe, some deep understanding can help to remove those billowing clouds of hurt hovering over you so that the sun can come shining through in your souls, even in this rough holy course. Now that we know *what* we are going to do, *how* will we proceed in getting some sunshine in your souls?

The overall course objective is to develop in students critical awareness of the nature, methods, and purpose of your preaching function, so that you will be able to know when you are right and when you are wrong. Nature equals *what* preaching is. Method equals *how* preaching is. Purpose equals *why* preaching is.

Now, this objective has to do with the reason why we will be spending so much time in trying to gain a comprehensive idea of what preaching is all about, so that we can be in position to preach in divine light in every respect all the time. In a word, we need to be sure that we have some basic understanding of the *what*, the *how*, and the *why* of genuine preaching with an illuminated mind. We are going to spend a lot of time on this comprehensive consideration, to be sure that you grasp the proper concept of *what* preaching really is (its nature), and *how* to go about the task of preaching effectively (its method), and *why* we must be engaged in this nasty business of preaching in the first place (its purpose).

All of this pondering over the ends and outs of preaching is so that we can be preaching in divine light in every respect every time we mount that pulpit. Ain't no ignorant monkey got no damn business with its dumb buncom-buncom up there in the pulpit in the first place, if he/she is not preaching in divine light. I don't give a damn if you are ordained or not. If you are not preaching with divine light, you ain't got no business with your ass up there. You need to have your ass down on the ground if you ain't got no more divine light than the rest of the folk in the pews. So get your dumb ignorant ass down from up there. In a hurry! Cause it ain't got no business up there whether you are ordained or not if it ain't preaching in divine light when you are up there. We need someone up there preaching in divine light, in every respect all the time. God didn't call anybody up there to be spreading darkness among folk.

Now, this Christian endeavor to make sure (say Amen, just because I cuss a little bit doesn't mean that I am not telling the truth) that we always preach in divine light in every respect has some serious implications for us here. For one thing it means that there is an ultimate concern here to prevent us from being at ease.

Now, some of us agree with that last statement too easily.

Sometimes—in fact, most of the time—we will find ourselves just like Isaiah in the temple during his conversion experience. In a genuine conversion experience, we will find that not only we ourselves have been wrong, but we live with and have been nurtured by and have been brainwashed in a religious culture that was also wrong. Dead wrong under God! That is why you have so many crazy, cockeyed, fallacious, down-right stupid religious notions running around in your young peanut heads now. Crazy religious notions that need challenging in the name of God. Some of those notions that you were raised on by loved ones are wrong. Dead wrong under God! And we need to get rid of those poisonous religious notions before they kill us religiously under our God.

So in addition to giving a full account of yourselves in communicative depth, you also need to justify every issue in terms of theological depth as well. You need to justify what you *laks* or don't *laks* on a divine theological basis of the whole. And no longer can you assess an issue merely on the basis of what mama, pop, and the folks back home taught you about religion. No longer can you do that.

They taught us many good things that were divine. We need to admit that and be grateful to them for it. But we also need to admit and not be grateful for the fallacies they taught us also, which are some bad things that must not abide, and such must be gotten rid of in the Lord's name. We *lak* many crazy things under God because we have been trained and drilled and brainwashed by a sinful, stupid religious culture back home by loved ones.

And I know why some of you like a little funkmaking in the service, even though you know that it doesn't make any sense. I know why you *laks* it because you were raised on it. It was the backspring for your lives all of your lives. Not because it is right or because it has any meaning, but you were raised on it, that is why you *laks* it. I know also why you need to get rid of it. It will kill you. It will either make a religious leader or a jackleg out of you in reference to what you do about it in God's name. So this is another thing we need to be perfectly clear about.

What I am saying is that I recognize that most of you came with limited ideas, but let me say this, in Jesus' name this morning, the situation is not hopeless. It is bad, but it is not hopeless, because I will endeavor to help some lost young souls by means of our holy exams to be born again of God this year. I demand in the name of God in your sermon preparation that you justify the issues as a saving means of grace for lost young souls being born again of God in this course this year. And we intend to give you lots and lots of graceful practice in justifying the issues theologically. We intend to demand in the name of God that you take some issues to court and prove theologically *what* and *how* and *why* you do or do not *laks* those issues in Jesus' name.

So, another thing that we need to be perfectly clear about on this justifying issue is to speak in theological depth for the welfare of black folks. Justifying is always in the light of that basic question of theologically justifying concerns. People do need to hear the *what*s and the *how*s and the *why*s in a deep theological sense, if we endeavor to speak with people by the wayside of life for them to make living divine decisions in reconciliation to their God.

Well now, if we expect for you to be justifying discussional questions in both communicative and theological depth in all of your sermon preparations, if we expect all of that of you, then it is obvious to most of you, we are deliberately putting a heavy cross on your shoulders. This makes it most obvious to the highest heavens that somebody is trying to pull a double-cross on you, doesn't it? So if all of you are clear of these facts by now, then I know what is happening in your minds.

You have some serious question in your mind like this: *WHY?* Isn't that the question? You know the *what* and the *how*, but *why*, Doc are you going to be so hard on us in this homiletics course? *Why* you going to treat us like we some kind of dog in our sermon preparation? *Why* you going to act like our name is some kind of old, mangy Rover the dog, Doc? *Why*, Doc? We ain't no dog. This class ain't suppose to be no dog show. So *why*, tell me, *why* you are going to act like we are Rover the dog? *Why?* There show nuff ain't no dogs in this class.

Well now, the reason why I will try my level best, deliberately, to treat you like you some kind of dog on these homiletical assignments has to do with my ultimate concern for your personal well-being, by means of this sure-fire integrative process of decision making on your preaching homework so that you will not be fumbling around the rest of your lives split in the valley of indecision. For it is not uncommon for young preachers and old preachers too to experience split persons in their being. It is not uncommon to find the average young preachers humping around this campus with their young preacher-being split, split with some new ideas, running around in their educated head coming from professors, and at the same time clinging to those old bad ideas in their uneducated heart from loved ones back home. Thus, a lot of young preachers have a kind of unresolved, warlike, battle-fatigue split in their being—having on the one hand new ideas in their heads, and on the other hand old ideas in their hearts, in direct collision with each other.

A whole lot of young preachers in seminary are split in their being. Just like Legions, the crazy man that met Jesus one day, struck with a thousand impulses, telling you to do any and everything foolish and crazy. You don't know what you are going to do. You can go a thousand ways with every impulse having as much power as the next. Totally disintegrated, in that, there is no central element. Everything is on its own, doing its own thing. You are split, split in school, split at home, split at church, split even when you get in the pulpit. Split! Split! Split! Split even in this preaching class. Split! Split!

And when there is a split in your being so high that one can't get over it and so deep that one can't get under it and so wide that one can't get around it, when that is happening in the soul, then nothing else but a definite commitment of the will can aid in divine willingness decision making and save you. Nothing but a dip down into the valley of decision can enable you to overcome that eternal split in your beings in depth.

I deliberately intend to lead you to the valley of decision in all of your preaching. That is exactly why I am going to treat you like you some kind of dog in this homiletics course so that you can get accustom to reconciling your head and heart through practice in positive decision making on your holy assignments. It will take everything that you know to make decisions in your sermon development and preaching preparation.

And for more quality matter, because of what this justifying process can mean to you personally, in your soul, let me prophesy

this, that somebody here, somebody right here in this class, is
going to be singing this song in his/her soul, after, not during, but
after it is all over. Somebody is going to be singing, "At the cross,
at the cross, where I first saw the light, and the burdens of my heart
rolled away, it was there by faith, I received my sight and now I am
happy all the day."

And somebody else might sing this song: "A prayer change in
my life has been wrought since Clark helped bring Jesus to my
heart. Oh what a joy floods my soul, and the storm billows rolled,
since Clark helped bring Jesus to my heart. Oh the joy of my soul
and the sea billows roll . . ."

And some more persons will say, "Holy, holy, holy." This cross
is not due to hate but to the contrary. The cross in this preaching
course represents the deepest meaning of God in the deepest theological sense. Love in the deepest theological sense always comes
with a cross mingled with it. That is why the cross is the symbol
that we wear. God's love has a cross in it. In the deepest theological sense, we are going to lead you again and again to Calvary. We
will lead you there out of our deepest concern for your personal
well-being in the name of our heavenly Father whose will is to
bruise you for your salvation in all of your holy sermons.

3

A—Not The, but A— Theological Interpretation of Preaching

Preaching is divine activity wherein the Word of God is proclaimed or announced on contemporary issues for an ultimate response to our God.

WE ARE NOW LOCATED on a leg of our homiletical journey called knowledge, which is midway between understanding and implementation. We find ourselves symbolically on the banks of the Jordan, after having made the trek across the desert of understanding, heading for the preaching promised land of implementation. So many of us here have sinned mightily against the Lord all the way across the desert of understanding, with Jehovah's wrath having visited some of those buried in the desert. Others committed sins of playing hooky, playing sleepy, playing with the material when they should have been present, awake, and ready to learn of God. A few folk experienced Jehovah's wrath through snake biting and lion mauling. The rest of us need to thank God for God's amazing grace, for sparing the rest of us *sinnahs*, even though we know that some more funerals are inevitable.

In order to comprehend the meaning of our present preaching experience, let us build two secure life rafts of knowledge for crossing this river safely. Life Raft #1 is a theological interpretation of preaching regarding God's stake in it. Life Raft #2 is the sociopsychological interpretation of homiletics regarding humans' stake in it. These two rafts will enable us to cross the Jordan River to the Preaching Promised Land, where we all *gon' un-lax wit' De Lawd runnin' things in De Lawd's* own holy way.

Now, the problem facing us here in the beginning is our need for agreement on a common definition of preaching, since so many Christians mean different things by preaching. The scene at the Annual Conference, our big meeting, is that preaching is simply trash blowing in on us from everywhere, especially when the bishop turns a *preachin' thaing* loose, saying, *"sic em,"* and *IT sicking* us.

Now, if our preaching definition has any theological validity to it at all, and I believe that it does, because you ain't dealing with no funkmaking theologian, you are dealing with one who got his doctorate in the subject of theology. We ain't doing no funkmaking when we talk about theology. I don't want to teach a course in theology because I see the relevance of it in preaching. I don't have to go back to teaching theory any more. When I bring that theology stuff over here in preaching, I can make a definition that is theologically sound. Just remember, you are not dealing with no jackleg in this area. You ain't got to run to any other theologian, if you want to know something about theology, then come in here.

So, an analysis of our preaching definition comprehensively goes like this. *What* is preaching?—substantially it is *divine activity. How* does preaching exist?—it exists in terms of the *Word of God proclaimed or announced on contemporary issues. Why* does preaching exist?—it is the way for *ultimate response to our God.* And your holy assignment is that everybody learn that preaching definition by heart this day, so that you do not sleep in sin or wake up in hell. Our task is to clean up preaching things around here with a broom and shovel, with a mop and bucket, with lye soap and plenty of hot water.

Therefore, since we desire, once and for all times, to clean up this messy situation about the concept of preaching in the minds of Christian brethren and *sisteren* fellowship, let us discuss at length a working, clarifying definition of the term "preaching," by means of analyzing each part of the recommended hypothesis, to prove its validity beyond a reasonable doubt, with the hope that the whole group will subscribe to it with some degree of consensus for a fellowship of kindred minds, whenever we mention that holy term called "preaching" in the name of our Lord.

DIVINE ACTIVITY

In order for us to grasp *divine activity*, the first element in our definition of preaching, we must expel from many minds a fallacy about the foundations of preaching, or forever smell a bad odor. A fallacy is a unique kind of error; it always seems to be true on the surface, but is always false in depth, and it is put out by jacklegs for catching unsuspecting suckers by the carloads. A preaching fallacy is equating *divine activity* with nasty collars turned around backward for so long historically, that we come to think of the preaching business as belonging to us humans rather than to God. Another preaching fallacy assumes the human voice to be *divine activity*, wherein monkeys have been fixing-it so long historically, that we come to think of preaching as being some kind of noise rather than power. Our positive concern is to set the record straight in the preaching drama—God alone, rather than humans and the human voice, is the prime factor, because God alone can preach without us.

Examples of God preaching without humans can be found in the Psalms, "heavens telling glory of God, earth showing handiworks." God speaks to Moses through a burning bush. God speaks to Elijah through silence in a cave. There are historical references to God preaching by God-self from Abraham to yours truly.

The implications of *divine activity* are twofold. Based on our ministerial responsibility, it is easy to fall into this fallacy, in that the Word is nigh unto us on that preaching stage, meaning that we ourselves must keep in mind who the real star of the preaching show is, and that we must remind others who want to worship us that the work is all divine. In addition, our ministerial responsibility requires that we be aware that preaching is really a reenactment of the original creation story, where God moves over the void and the chaos in our lives calling for the dawning of a new day, with the Holy One of Israel being the one who claims, judges, persuades, convinces, and convicts us as God's own preacher.

We need to teach the folk that preaching is done by God alone rather than by some funkmaking minstrel, which is the basic reason for emphasizing at the very beginning of our definition that preaching is substantially *divine activity*. And, preaching justice will best be served, if the jury finds those minstrel funkmakers guilty and sentences them to be hanged, so that those menaces to people experiencing *divine activity* will be banished from the preaching affairs of God forever.

PROCLAIMED OR ANNOUNCED

I am dealing with the third element in the definition of preaching, *proclaimed or announced*, before dealing with the second element, *Word of God*, out of a deliberate concern to show the distinctive roles of the divine and human activities in close connection, in order to get the roles straight. Because we still hear about preaching contests and crowning human preachers *"kaing"* in the *cullud ir-religious* community, including even this so-called intellectual *cullud* seminary, I am discussing this consideration, "proclaimed or announced," second.

The literal meaning of proclaimed is *pro,* a prefix meaning "for, in favor of, in behalf of," *claim,* the root meaning "to own or be the owner." The implications of *proclaimed or announced* for us as ministers is that we are agents, stewards, representatives, and caretakers for the owner. We are not the big boss but the straw bosses. *Us is 'posed to be de foremen(ses)* around here. We are not the sponsors of the preaching program. Like Ed McMann, we say, "Heeeeeeeere's Johnny!"

The word minister comes from *mini,* meaning "little," *ster,* "official." Prophet comes from *pro,* meaning "for," *phet,* meaning "to say." Pronounce comes from *pro,* meaning "for," *nounce,* meaning "to say." Thus, to *proclaim/announce* has to do with the role of human agents in the divine preaching drama, relative to our being deliverers of the will and intent of our heavenly king to the people, so that the people can know and heed and obey our heavenly king.

The historical significance of proclaimers of old has to do with the divine rights of kings. In the days of kings, kings were conceived of as being ordained by God to be owners of all things and persons in the kingdom. Monarch comes from *mon,* meaning "one," and *arch*, meaning "ruler." The combined meaning is one who is to rule over everything and everybody. Sometimes the king would make his will known by dictating to scribes to write it down right. At other times, the king would put a seal of approval on something written to make it official. And oftentimes the king called in proclaimers to deliver official orders from place to place and to read it right for the subjects to heed and obey.

The caution of proclaimers of old, those with honorable retirement, is that the proclaimers of old should never try to get fancy in trying to be fixin' it nicely and get the people confused about what to put their attention on. Their job was to tell it like it was. The proclaimers of old were not to take a chance on losing the official message and be out among the king's people trying to 'member a lost message, rolling their eyeballs up to the sky, talking about, "I think or guess or *'magine*, or *reg'n* the king said. . . ."

Likewise, the contemporary implication for us as proclaimers is that we require conferences with our king; it is necessary for us to steal away in a programmed way for prayer and meditation, so that people will be aware that their heavenly king has spoken to us first, in order for them to be convinced that they need to obey our proclaimed/announced orders. If we seriously want to express the Christian message with power, we must make prayer and meditation a living part of our beings. Every day we must sit by ourselves alone to do some thinking on the issues to gain the insight needed for effective preparation. Every day we must kneel by ourselves alone to do some dialoguing with God for divine power for effective proclamation.

Some *younguns* may respond, "Naw, Man!! I don't go for all that rump and knee stuff Doc is putting down. I can do without it. Just show me where the platform is, and I will show you what I can do." We all know what you can do without prayer and meditation based on your own funkmaking facts. So that ain't the real question. What we really want to know is, What could you do with it? In essence, authoritative speaking requires that we recognize that we have the divine right to speak to people with conviction *if* we have the official seal of our heavenly King on our message and on our proclaimed being.

In the Bible, Jesus claims that he always speaks as one having authority in his being. *Exousia* means "from, out of, the being or soul." Nicodemus said to Jesus, "We know that you truly must be a man from God." No man does or says such things unless God be with him, or he's crazy.

When it comes to *proclaiming/announcing*, the false words are "I think, suppose, guess, imagine, and reckon." They should be overruled in the preaching court. The true words are "I know, I am persuaded, and thus saith the Lord." Sustained. My response to your sinful objection—"Sounds dogmatic," so you say. Well, how else is truth supposed to be spoken except dogmatically?

WORD OF GOD

The general meaning of *Word of God*, the second element in the definition of preaching, has to do with the content of the Gospel being proclaimed—holy stuff being delivered to needy people for the purpose of feeding hungry souls the manna most satisfying. The *Word of God* is not the Bible, but God as God-self. I need to make a declaration at the outset for killing off a fallacy commonly held by a lot of Christians, namely, that the Bible is the *Word of God*. The probable reason for this fallacy is the close association of the Bible and preaching, especially the custom of starting off with a biblical text. We should not say, *"Women and Men, I present to y'all dis holy book as God's Word, kotin' and 'peatin' a whole lot of it."* Instead, we proclaim, "Ladies and Gentlemen, I present to you God as God-self, to heal you and bless you as God-self— Immanuel in preaching!"

Word of God as Gospel

The literal meaning of *gospel* is an elision of the words *God* and *spell*. "Elision" means that some of the letters drop out of the original words when two or more words are joined together to be one word. The composite meaning of *Gospel* refers to a time or season or spell when it is proclaimed that God-is-with-us-now for blessing us. Immanuel! Yes, the *Gospel* is significant because it is Good News, since God's presence always means things changing and straightened out for the better. There is a singing expression about "good news, chariot's coming"—God's in the chariot. Isaiah says, "Comfort ye! Comfort ye! Make straight in the desert a highway for your God" so that God can get here faster. And Jesus' expression, "Blessed are you!"—*Cause Ah is hyah!*

Word of God as Grace

In the Gospel of John, Jesus is described as "full of grace and truth." Generally, *grace* means that we receive something from another, which we have no right or claim to, thus evoking thanks for it—a free gift, a pure favor, a boon. Historically, in the days of the kings, when the king was considered divinely ordained to be the sole owner of everything and everybody, *grace* was when the king gave things solely at his good pleasure—a king's boon. In the Spanish language, *gracias* means "thank you" for this gift. In the New Testament, *grace* has to do with the content of the gospel, in terms of proclaiming the unmerited granting by God to desperately sinful people of forgiveness of sin and the power to overcome sin. The purpose of this grace is to make it possible for people to have right relations with their God again with fellowshipping power—a consideration that can best be understood in the light of understanding human sin.

Human sin is nothing new for anyone here. The principle of sin is always being basically rebellious, defiant, arrogant in trying to take over in God's kingdom, basically against God. The characteristics of sin always involve some kind of self-deception and lying, such as, "That snake force me to do it!" "That woman did, too!" Or, "God must have wanted a little sin because God put it there and made me want it!"

Some of the obvious symptoms of sinful nature can be found in our *missin' res'* at night, often *tossin'* and *turnin'* all night or having nightmares when we do fall asleep, not because of something we *et* neither, but because of something we are. Other symptoms have to do with us *lookin'* at folks either *lak* we just stole something or hiding behind sunshades, not because of *needin'* no eyeglasses neither, but because of something we are. A social characteristic of sin is its epidemic nature, through a recruitment campaign to drag others in to defeat the enemy—G-O-D! And in turn, we need to be lynched without a trial, as the wages of sin cause us to live on the edge of God's kingdom, duckin' and hidin' in the bushes away from the presence of an angry God.

The basic content of the gospel is that *grace* is forgiveness and power, wherein pardon, amnesty, and friendship are proclaimed in a convincing way, so that sinners can begin to believe that it is safe to come out of hiding and live again in God's presence, if sinners will repent. *Grace*, as empowerment, is when we proclaim divine aid and assistance in convincing ways, so that sinners will begin to partake of God's vitamins, in order to move out of the ghetto of sin, repent, and do as Apostle Paul advocates, "Go on to make Christ our own."

Word of God as Truth

A haunting question raised along the way is, What is truth? *Ordinary truth* has to do with the relation of our words to the facts of existence, with the facts determining whether truth or lies are being spoken. Tellin' it! *Theological truth* has to do with the relation of the facts of existence to the Word of God, with the Word of God determining whether truth or lies are being lived. Bein' it!

The universal standard of *theological truth* is the intent and purpose of the Creator God as the sole test of what should or should not be in God's creation, institutionally, community-wise, nationally, or internationally. The individual standard of *theological truth* is the specific intent and purpose of the Creator God in endowing each individual with unique talents and abilities and temperaments for making special contributions to/in life.

Untruth emerges when we refuse to accept what we really have and who we really are, out of resentment against God for not having given us all the gifts in creation. Some of us are natural carpenters, claiming the call to the *ministry-of-the-woid* rather than being a *minister-of-the-wood*, after all, it's only human. Others of us are little fish who desire foolishly to be *lak* the contented sea cow beside the sea rather than living naturally in the sea.

Truth is the basic content of the gospel, in terms of proclaiming the will and intent of the Creator God, for the meaning of our individual and institutional existence, so that we, creatures, can make living, creative adjustments to that divinely declared content. The meaning of *Jesus Christ as Truth* is found in the very essence of Jesus' coming to place us flippin' and floppin' creatures back in relation to our true selves again. Yes, Jesus is the way, the truth, and the life.

CONTEMPORARY ISSUES

Contemporary Issues, the fourth element of the recommended definition of preaching, has to do with the relevant, existential context, the real-life situation to which the gospel is addressed, relating the gospel concretely to problems burdening people down beyond human repair, helping people to overcome in the ultimate sense of the term. The relevant, existential context bears upon the living needs of people here and now, in terms of some divine blessing in the currently killing conditions, since the genuinely theological must relate to the sociological, and the genuinely vertical must relate to the horizontal. The real-life situation is relative to the question, "Is there any balm in Gilead to heal my wounded, sin-sick soul?" so that the gospel will be focused on living issues.

The significance of *contemporary issues* is that it is the part of our preaching where many ministers often fail miserably. An instance of white jackleg irrelevance occurred in a downtown Birmingham church where Dr. Martin Luther King, Jr., was leading a campaign for freedom in 1963. In the midst of fire hose, biting dogs, and police brutality, this white jackleg *paahstuh* preached on the subject, "How to Grow Old Gracefully."

Black jackleg irrelevance can be found in the frequent preoccupation with something dead or foolish as it relates to using or abusing the meaning of the Bible in a most irrelevant manner. During a *cullud* revival week, a jackleg on the first night preached on *"Jacob and de' long lader to heav'm."* (So what???) Second night: *"Moses and de' divided water for walkin'."* (So what???) Third night: *"Jesus and de' walkin on water."* (So what???) Last night: *"Jesus and de great-big hoit."* (So what? I still ask.) My intent is not to be sacrilegious but to raise the question of the relevance of the gospel to the problems of the people here and now for blessing. People must see the connection between what happened and their particular needs. The jackleg in the revival was killin' people's spirits, since people are really interested in the question Does God save? rather than in the question Did God save long ago?

The question of relevance is of utmost significance. Ain't no use in expecting to have a relevant church for saving others unless the church members themselves have been saved first. Unsaved members can't be expected to be nice and save others for Christ, since they are only human.

Another significant implication of relevance is the generalized fallacy that aspirin tablets can cure everything, and that religious aspirin can cure every religious ailment, such as "pray and hold on!" Say, for instance, you go to the doctor with your side *killin' ya*. The medical doctor responds with a generalized prescription about going home, taking some aspirin, getting in bed, and waiting to see what gon' happen. Your ailing response, being your thoughts on religion, might be that you are not paying that monkey for no services rendered in really healing you. Or, you might even hit that monkey for no services rendered as you wait for death. Ain't no use in expecting generalized prescriptions to solve all problems faced, if no specific solutions are suggested from the pulpit.

Moreover, *contemporary issues* are important because most people do indeed desperately need God's help right now. They need to be fed the gospel with some Good News in it for their weary souls right now, on this side of the Jordan. Hellish problems are driving people further and further away from their God, further and further away from their own selves, at every turn in the road today. Living today is a living hell for most people, with hell-fire blazing in and around their souls.

That is why we say that preaching is substantially divine activity, wherein the Word of God (as Good News) must be proclaimed or announced on living, burning, hellish, contemporary issues, with a view toward helping desperately needy people to really overcome here and now, on this side of the Jordan, through responding to the Creator who is our God, and who is also our very present helper in times of deep trouble on this side of the Jordan, right here and right now.

For you young preachers, this does not mean that you take every issue to the pulpit that affects only a few people in the congregation. For instance, a feud over your salary is indeed a contemporary issue, but an issue that should be settled in the business meeting and not in the pulpit, where the preacher has an unfair advantage. A member caught in adultery is indeed a contemporary issue, but it is an issue that should be settled in the counseling chamber and not be broadcast from the pulpit. What I mean is that you take any issue to the pulpit that affects the congregation as a whole, overall sins affecting all people, such as identity crises, home crises, educational crises, youth crises, political crises, and social crises, especially racism.

ULTIMATE RESPONSE TO OUR GOD

The meaning of *ultimate response*, the fifth and final element in the definition of preaching, has to do with the divine objective of the gospel proclamation, wherein there is a call for a reaction to the claims and demands of God in genuine preaching, for either entering into or growing up in the kingdom of God through a positive decision. A positive reaction is to decide to do, or to feel, or to think, or to be something holy and different in relation to our Maker. It is either a yea or an irresponsible nay to the holy claims (ownership) and righteous demands (obedience) of God in the genuine gospel, since there is no neutral ground for a maybe. Neutrality cannot prevail where genuine preaching takes place. By nature, it always does one of two things—either draws people into the arms of God or drives them further into their sins.

Some fallacy thinkers have misconceptions of the *what-how-why* of gospel preaching, thus fallaciously thinking that the thing to do most of all is beat everybody to the door in order to block it to get *ouvr* merited applause for such a lovely presentation that morning. Others who are success seekers need to realize that if we get 100-percent applause from everybody all the time, then either our heavenly Father is not enjoying our earthly success or we have some big *liahs* passing by us at that sanctuary door. Gospel preaching is not a verbal treat given for parishioners to get their kicks like the entertainment from a Flip Wilson clown on that preaching stage. Gospel preaching is a verbal treatment given for cancerous surgery, like the operations in a hospital.

Evidence of *ultimate response* resentment is found in that Birmingham white church with that white jackleg actually playing the ropes like a champion on that irrelevant subject about graceful gerontology. Many black *paastuhs* actually play those same ropes like champions too, on those irrelevant subjects about somebody's dear old mama in a lonely graveyard many, many miles away. In the tradition, there is a whole culture of *cullud preachin'* that has been hatched as a means of dealing with *cullud* resentment, wherein big-time jackleg *preechahs* advise—"Don't let them fool you. Preaching ain't nothing but organized hollering!!" And in turn, young *preechahs* buy into this fallacy and want *homi-ca-let-ics* to give more techniques on the ways of better funkmaking.

Therefore, as a possible resource for inspiring young preachers, I appeal to Jesus Christ, since Jesus Christ founded a tradition of truth-making rather than funkmaking, which is why Jesus Christ was crucified. The common so-called unrighteous heard Jesus gladly. The elite so-called righteous heard Jesus madly. Also, I appeal to human need, since weary and sin-sick people need to be led home-to-God for some soul-rest-in-God. All in all, I appeal on the basis of Jesus' promise as a possible resource for inspiring young preachers to use the most communicative kinds of human expressions for convincing and persuading women, men, and children, since Jesus Christ said, "I, even I, will be with you to support you every step of the way to victory."

4

A Critique of Contemporary Preaching

Clark's critique of contemporary preaching is a ministerial indictment that much of our preaching has been either light or lying or both, wherein far too many of us have slung together some spiritual slop callously or carelessly, late on Saturday night or early on Sunday morning, with the inevitable consequence of parishioners running from church to church, hollering and knocking over benches in search of genuine food for their souls.

WITH OUR PRACTICAL DEFINITION IN MIND—preaching is divine activity, wherein the Word of God is proclaimed or announced on a contemporary issue with an ultimate response to our God—and with you looking like and acting like you know that you ain't through with the definition of preaching yet, we are now in position to give our attention to a new issue that we will be wrestling with in this lecture, "a critique of contemporary preaching." We will endeavor to use our working theological definition of preaching as a background for making a contemporary critique. We will use what we now understand about preaching to make a critical judgment on preaching today. You do indeed need to have some idea of where you now stand in relation to this preaching business, so that you can have some idea of what you must be doing in the future as aspiring preachers. You must assess the preaching situation in the present, so that you can know what the future preaching situation calls forth from you. Ain't no sense in trying to carve out a preaching future unless you know what the preaching score is now on the contemporary scene, because your preaching future is based on the preaching situation existing now in the contemporary context.

For instance, if you find the existing preaching situation today to be sound, then you merely need to build upon that sound foundation in your future endeavors. If there is a sound foundation then just build on it. But, if you find that the existing preaching situation is full of honky-donk in the present, then you need to recognize that you will have to clean up that bad situation at the very beginning of your future endeavors. If you got honky-donk on the scene, then you got to clean it away. Every act in the future is based on the present reality. Thus, we need to make an honest critique of the present preaching situation so that you can know how to get started in the future endeavors of your preaching ministry.

And we especially want to make an honest critique of the black preaching situation, since we are definitely interested in the meaning and implications of preaching for future black liberation. You got to know what you got to do if you are about liberation. We definitely want to see *what* and *how* and *why* preaching can help black folks to really overcome in this land of ours through our preaching.

Without prejudicing the case completely beforehand, let me say that you will definitely need some hip boots and dungarees in your future ministry. You ain't going to need no suit and no tie, no robe and no high heels, to do a relevant job in your future preaching ministry. Because any time you are working in an outhouse, any time you are wading in piles and piles of do-do, you definitely need hip boots and dungarees rather than a suit and a tie or robes and high heels to do that kind of work. Don't think that your main job is with a suit and tie, or robes and high heels, when you get started. It ain't. I don't want to prejudice the case, but I need to alert you to the kind of clothes you will need to wear. If you are really interested in helping black folks to overcome through some powerful preaching, then let us make a threefold critique of the contemporary situation of preaching.

First of all, we will make a general assessment of the preaching situation in mainline Protestantism in America. Second, we will endeavor to prove that our general assessment is accurate by calling in some unimpeachable witnesses to testify before the judge and the jury. And third, we will give some didactic causes for the bad situation on the present preaching scene. Three things we got to do. We are going to give you an assessment of how things are. We are going to prove it. And then we are going to tell you why it is like it is. So, let us begin with this necessary critique, for liberation purposes, by making this general assessment in the light of our working definition of preaching.

If our definition of preaching has any theological validity at all—and it does—and if there is any virtue in it for your usage—and I believe that it has that—then our definition should make us acutely aware of a serious indictment against much that parades around under the disguise of preaching in our midst today. For many of those preaching impostors need to be arrested for impersonating genuine proclaimers of the Most High. Much of contemporary preaching is like what Albert Knudson said about contemporary theology in his time. For the most part, not every part, but for the most part, for the predominant part, preaching is "shallow and in the shadows."

Now, by assessing much of contemporary preaching as being shallow, we mean that much of so-called preaching today is not getting at the deep, fundamental, serious questions of life that people are concerned about. Much contemporary preaching is often lacking divine depth and human depth. No sound theology is in it and no understanding of sound psychology or sociology is under it. There is often no great import, divine or human, in much of today's crap-trap. There is often no profound impact on the thinking and behavior of people in their living today. In that sense, much of today's preaching is about as deep as a single dewdrop on the desert sand at high noon, shallow. Pish! There is a drop of dew out there, but you don't even know that it is out there.

Now, by assessing much of contemporary preaching as being in the shadows, we mean that most people today don't normally take preaching seriously. Thus, preaching today is no longer in the limelight as it once was, but it is often more or less a sidelight in church. Like the monkey that ask me, "Do you think that we ought to have some drama?" Yes, I think we ought to have it on Sunday evening, when you are going to have some kind of program, but not in the place of preaching. "Do you think that we ought to have a cantata at 11:30 on Sunday morning?" Hell no! Hell no! If it were not for preaching, you wouldn't have a church. I am talking about the things that brought the church into existence. Some people are now putting preaching aside so that we can have a songfest. Yes, there is gospel in music. And there is gospel in drama, nobody is denying that. All we are saying is that music and drama did not bring the church into existence, and it ain't going to keep it in existence.

Don't let no devil fool you out of your place in the pulpit. There is only one time when the devil ought to fool you out of the pulpit, and that is when you ain't got no message. Sit down and let the choir take over, for maybe they can sing some gospel. If you got your message ready, like you ought to have it ready, then you tell the choir that they have their part. Let the choir sing, and you don't want no whole lot of humming and no organ playing while you are trying to preach the gospel, talking about needing some help. If you ain't got your sermon ready, then let the organ drown you out.

Let's be sure, what I am saying is that preaching is more on the sidelines today. People are asking questions about whether they even need a preacher. And even preachers talking about, you think that we ought to have drama instead of a sermon. You need to be sure that preaching is still a part of our cultural heritage. No one denies that. And most people today would be upset with a drama or cantata if we did do it every Lord's day.

For the most part, contemporary preaching is something being done for the record only. It is something for the sake of religious appearances. We can't have a service without preaching. What would the folk outside say? So much of today's preaching is about keeping up our religious image, but it is actually nothing to get serious about for most people today, including jacklegs with nasty collars on backwards.

Preaching is often shallow and in the shadows, often some kind of shady affair in the shadows even for many with nasty collars on backwards. You can tell that by the time preachers give to preparing to preach. Some fools think that they can get a sermon together in two or three hours. They are crazy. It will take the average one of you, if you really do it right, it will take you about forty to sixty hours. It takes me twenty hours to get all these lectures together.

It takes me twenty hours to get a decent sermon out. Did you know that? Yes, it does. Every lecture that you receive means that you got twenty hours of me, every time I come before you up here. And, if I got these ideas and concepts internalized, and I got to put my sentences together automatically, then I know what kind of time it is going to take you. Night and day, wrestling with an angel until day breaks and the Lord blesses you.

So that is my general assessment of the preaching situation in mainline Protestantism in contemporary America. Generally speaking, it is most definitely shallow and in the shadows. It is shallow in content as it relates to the deep issues in contemporary life. And it is definitely in the shadows in interest as it relates to being significant to most people trying to find answers to problems of life here and now. Most people, when they got problems, they don't even think about the preacher any more. The preacher is that fellow who gets up there and talks real light and doesn't know anything.

Well now, why Doc talking about preaching that-a way? Doc must be mad at the world talking like that. How can Doc say a nasty thing like that about his brethren of the cloth? Something definitely must be wrong with Doc talking about preaching being shallow and in the shadows. Listen brothers and sisters, let me tell you about it. I know what Doc's problem is, so let me tell you all about Doc. [Now, when you run into a fool talking like that, then you know that he ain't got no damn sense. It is not that he is thinking wrong, it is that he ain't got no thought and trying to get one.] *See, Doc is upset about one of two things. See I know what makes a man talk like that, talking the way that Doc is talking. It is either one of two problems that he got. So let me tell you all about Doc's problem.*

On one hand, a man talks like that because of his frustrated vocational ambitions, talks like that when he did not get what he wanted in life. And you see Doc always wanted to be a bishop in his church. You know, all AME preachers want to be bishops and Doc ain't never been elected as a delegate to General Conference. Doc can't even make it as a delegate. He has been ordained twenty-five years and he can't even make delegate.

So on one hand [You know these are fool lies. I ain't never been a delegate because I never ran. I have always been on my own turf trying to teach fools like you. This fool acts like this is the truth coming out. All of this is a lie.], *it could be Doc's frustration with AME politics that causes Doc to talk that way about preaching being shallow and in the shadows.*

On the other hand, a man talks like that also because of sexual frustration. A man talks like that also when he needs some good loving in his life. Good loving changes things and makes a man see things differently. Some good loving would straighten Doc out. It would make Doc see things differently about the preaching situation. Cause I know. I know that good loving changes things, makes a man see things differently.

You see brothers and sisters, I knows all about sexual frustration, because I use to go around sexually frustrated myself. I used to go around mad at the world until I seed the light. Because one day, one day the heavens opened to me. And one day, one day it all became clear to me. One day the heavens opened and I seed things clearly for the first time in my life. So let me tell you about what happened to me. One day, things changed for me, heaven opened up, and I remember that blessed day. It was like it was just yesterday.

I left home early one morning on my way to work. I was sad in my heart and I was mad at the world. And then on my way to work, the lightning flashed and the thunder rolled and I heard a voice saying something to me on my way to work. It said, Son, Son, I know that your heart is heavy, and there is sadness in your heart on your way to work. Son, Son, I got a blessing for you that is going to make everything alright. Son, Son let me tell you what I want you to do. Son, I want you to go down to big-leg Susie's house because I got something down there to put joy in your heart.

Maybe this seminarian does have a point. Maybe I do need to be taken to big-leg Susie's house to get a good piece of loving. I ain't going to argue against that. Nobody knows all about himself. It takes someone else, as I have said before, to see some things that we can't see about ourselves. Maybe my meanness and all my nasty talk are based on the fact that I need a good piece of loving. I will take that recommendation under serious advisement.

But now that I have heard your story, let me tell you something.

Even after, even after I get that good loving from big-leg Susie, I will still be saying that much of contemporary preaching is shallow. Even after I get some good loving, I will still be saying that much of today's preaching is shallow and in the shadows, fool.

And I will tell you something else, fool. Big-leg Susie would have to have some mighty good loving to convert all these witnesses I got lined up. We have a whole gang of witnesses lined up— all of whom have come forward gladly to testify in court that much of today's preaching is shallow and in the shadows, even so-called powerful black preaching, even in my own denomination.

So big-leg Susie would have to roll a whole lot of folks in her nasty brass bed to get all of these witnesses to see things differently, fool. And I don't believe that nobody's stuff is that good, at least not good enough to convert all of these witnesses on my side. So let's forget about good loving for the moment. Good loving ain't got a thing to do with what we are talking about at this time. Can't no sexual act perform the miracle of changing all this preaching do-do on the contemporary scene into no ice cream soda. So even after we all get that good loving, I will still say that much of contemporary preaching is shallow and in the shadows, if we assess it objectively. So it must have been a devil who was talking with you on your way to work, fool, because it sure wasn't the Lord. The Lord tells us that preaching today is shallow and in the shadows.

Well now, since I have set forth a serious indictment against so many preachers on the contemporary scene, I am under divine obligation to prove the charges or be liable for slander and defamation of preaching character. So I want to prove these charges in court by calling upon some unimpeachable witnesses. Now, this set of witnesses that we need to call will verify my indictment of today's preaching. And because time is of the essence, permit me to call upon my main witness at this time. We might call upon other witnesses, later if needed.

Now, our main witness, Billy Grahamism, came to my attention several years ago when he conducted a two-week revival crusade in Los Angeles. The thing that struck me was that at the particular crusade, there was an exceptionally large crowd participating. Graham always gathered a great big crowd, but that Los Angeles crowd was exceptionally large. Listen to these statistics.

That crusade in Los Angeles involved some 930,344 persons. Not nine thousand, but nine hundred and thirty thousand, three hundred and forty-four, almost a million folk involved in that crusade in Los Angeles during those two weeks. And listen to this, ladies and gentlemen of this jury, more than forty thousand souls, not four thousand souls, but more than forty thousand souls came streaming down that aisle in that crusade to accept Christ for the first time. Thousands streaming down those aisles coming to accept Christ with tears in their eyes.

Now hear this, most of those forty thousand converts, not just half of them, but most of those forty thousand converts, were already members of local churches, Your Honor. Most of those converts had sat listening to local pastors and felt absolutely nothing, unmoved, Sunday after Sunday. But now in that crusade, those same members did feel something and were moving down those aisles by the thousands. Why, Your Honor? Why Graham and not those local pastors, Your Honor?

Your Honor, and ladies and gentlemen of this jury, maybe lying pastors and those future lying pastors in the seminary will conjure up all kinds of lies to account for Billy Graham's apparent success as over against the obvious failures of pastors on the local level. They make up all kinds of great, big lies trying to make Graham's success look bad and their own failures look good, Your Honor.

So you will hear these kinds of lies being bellowed from local pastoral liars and their disciples in the seminary about Billy Graham's apparent success. Some will say, for instance, that it must be that many of those folks love to put on a great big shows and get converted in a large setting, trying to make a big deal about their conversion on television. They wouldn't be streaming down there except for the fact that the television cameras are on the scene. That is why he got so many and we don't get none.

Some others will say that it must be that Graham has some penny actors to start that flow down those aisles, and those forty thousand people were merely playing follow-the-leader unknowingly. He had some actors back there to start with the tears rolling down their cheeks, and the power of suggestion influenced others to follow their behinds. "If you get things started and end up having a whole lot of folks streaming down those aisles, here is fifty

A CRITIQUE OF CONTEMPORARY PREACHING

dollars for you. And as you come down the aisle it will throw a suggestion to the crowd and more people will follow." It must be that.

And still others might say that it must be Graham's brand of fundamentalism, always talking about the Bible and what the Bible says. He has a Bible in his hand that is capturing the religious right, the same way that the box brand of conservatism captured the segregationist right in 1966 and in 1970 in Georgia. The conservatives got the majority vote in 1970 because they appealed to the segregationists. I think that is what is happening with Graham holding the Bible up there. It is impressive and folks come.

And still others might come up with this great big lie, and this lie might have some disciples in this room. It must be, it has got to be the persuasion of the music from the thousand-voice choir that is doing the job. It must be the choir. It has got to be the choir because it can't be the preaching because preaching can't do that much. It is that thousand-voice choir that he got up there that is drawing those folk down the aisles, so much so that forty thousand folks came forward. It must be the choir that is doing that trick, because after all, more people get more gospel from the music than from the preaching in worship anyway, said one *cullud* pastor in fact, after messing up one Sunday morning.

The *cullud* pastor said this, knowing that I was sitting over there as the professor of homiletics. He said, "You know that I didn't do so well this morning but we had the choir anyway. And after all, more people get more out of what the musician does than what you do in your preaching class Doc." And the saddest part about that lying statement is that he did not even see that that statement was an indictment against him, talking about his insignificance.

Why should more people get more gospel from the choir than from the preacher, Your Honor? Why? Why would people get more out of the choir, untrained professionally, than from us who are suppose to be trained professionally, Your Honor? That was an indictment against preaching, not a compliment back to the choir.

It should be most obvious to this court that all those rationalized lies are supported by liars with nasty collars on backwards, so as to account for our preaching failure over against Graham's apparent success, Your Honor.

Now, Your Honor, and ladies and gentlemen of this jury, let me set the record straight about the prosecutor's personal attitude about Billy Graham. Let me set that record straight, Your Honor, because Billy Graham is not a specimen of a genuine prophet, as far as I as the prosecutor is concerned, your Honor. Billy Graham was too close to that lying Richard Nixon, and anybody friendly to Richard Nixon is automatically my personal enemy.

Your Honor, and ladies and gentlemen of this jury, we are not trying to prove that Billy Graham is the greatest and mostest. Your Honor, all that we are trying to prove by this witness is that most of our local members are spiritually hungry. Your Honor, and ladies and gentlemen of this jury, that is all that we are trying to prove by this witness. Not that we like Graham, but that what he is doing proves that people are hungry at the local level. And whether or not I like Billy Graham personally is not the issue, Your Honor. What really is the issue is that Billy Graham's apparent success proves conclusively that most people on the local level are being starved out spiritually by most local pastors. Those people are not getting enough, if anything at all, to eat spiritually in most local churches, Your Honor, and ladies and gentlemen of this jury. All those lies put out by lying local pastors and their lying seminary disciples against Billy Graham are simply not true, Your Honor. The simple truth of the matter is that those folks are simply starved at the local level. That is the most plausible explanation of all, Your Honor, and ladies and gentlemen of this jury.

Let me dramatize this spiritually hungry appetite of local folk to this court through a concrete personal illustration. Your Honor, and ladies and gentlemen of this jury, let me put this thing down on the ground so that everybody in this court can get it, so that you can reach a fair verdict on this issue of whether preaching is shallow and in the shadows. (Now this is the way you give examples in sermons.)

For example, where I once lived, my garbage cans were turned over almost every day by some hungry dogs, all because people in the neighborhood did not believe in feeding their dogs at home, Your Honor. They merely turned those dogs loose at suppertime to fend for themselves, Your Honor. So every day, Your Honor, every single day, every day, Your Honor, it was a sound being heard like this in my backyard. BAM DE BAM BAM BAMA BAMA LAMA RING RING RING with hungry dogs turning over my garbage cans looking for something to eat, Your Honor. Every day there were those hungry dogs looking for a meal and with garbage all over my back yard. Every day, Your Honor, BOOM DE BAM BAM, BAMA BAMA LAMA RING RING was in my backyard with garbage all over my yard. That was the way it was every day where I once lived, Your Honor, and ladies and gentlemen of this jury.

But where I now live, where I now live is an entirely different story. There are about twenty dogs in the community where I now live, Your Honor, so it ain't just about dogs. And up until last year, up until last year when the economic recession started, up until then, I did not have but six or seven incidents of overturned garbage cans in the past ten years in my present neighborhood, Your Honor, and ladies and gentlemen of this jury. Only six or seven overturned trash cans in ten years, but every day, every day before in my old neighborhood. Why, Your Honor? Why over-turned garbage cans every day before? And why not the same story now? The explanation should be obvious to this court, Your Honor.

It is because people in my present neighborhood feed their dogs at home. At least they did until Nixon started a recession last year, with inflation for dessert with a steady diet of recession. They would give those dogs something to eat at home and those garbage cans in my present neighborhood stayed erect. And the garbage men, the garbage men in both communities will gladly come to this court to verify that fact, Your Honor. The garbage men in my old neighborhood will tell you that the garbage cans are all over the yard, and the garbage men in my present neighborhood will tell you that very seldom, if ever, do you see garage cans turned over in my present neighborhood. If you don't believe me, I'll bring them into court, if you need them to testify.

So, Your Honor, and ladies and gentlemen of this jury, does that illustration not suggest a more plausible explanation of what is really happening in many, many local churches over against those lies put out against Graham by some local pastors? Those local pastors are frequently turning the hungry people loose Sunday after Sunday to turn over somebody's spiritual garbage cans, Your Honor, and ladies and gentlemen of this jury.

And like those hungry dogs in my past neighborhood, those church folks will head for anybody's spiritual garbage can to turn over looking for a spiritual meal. Also, Your Honor, and ladies and gentlemen of this jury, because like those hungry dogs in my past neighborhood, the present hungry folks in church know that there is nothing on the table. In fact, nothing is even cooking at home in the local parish with the local preacher. So, Your Honor, it is every man for himself.

And those hungry souls head for Billy Graham's or anybody else's spiritual garbage can to turn it over for some soul food for their starving selves. And those 930,344 souls at that Los Angeles crusade and those forty thousand souls streaming down those aisles who belong to our churches let the cat out of the bag about the spiritual poverty program in many, many local churches in this land, Your Honor, and ladies and gentlemen of this jury. That Los Angeles group let the whole world know what is happening in those spiritual dells on the local level, your Honor.

To tell you the truth, Your Honor, Billy Graham does not have to be in town to reveal the poverty in preaching in most local churches. You don't have to get a great big person like Billy Graham. Other lesser-likes, other people who ain't got no fame like Billy Graham can also let the cat out of the bag about the spiritual malnutrition in most local churches on the contemporary scene.

For instance, just let certain hummingbird clergy come to town, or get hold of a red-eyed drunken quartet from the alley, a bunch of bums with liquor on their breath hollering Mother, Mother, Mother, or just haul off a ten-year-old kid, doesn't even have to be a grown-up, a ten-year-old kid, just get a ten-year-old kid imitating a jackleg and all those lesser-likes will outdo the average local pastor and will have most of our hungry people out there at those jackleg services. They will be out there turning over garbage cans for a desperately needed spiritual meal, Your Honor, and ladies and gentlemen of this jury.

And let me tell you something else, even after folks leave us every Sunday morning—in fact, before they get to us—they turn on the radio. They know if they are going to get anything. They have got to turn on the radio if they are going to get some spiritual food that day. They know ain't nothing going to happen when they get to church. And when they leave church, what are they going to do? At night, they are going to be saying where, where is so-and-so jackleg preaching? When people are hungry they will go anywhere to try and get something to eat.

Your Honor, and ladies and gentlemen of this jury, the prosecutor respectfully requests your forgiveness and your indulgence for bringing the dead into this nasty situation. But I am sure that the critical nature of this case warrants desperate efforts to get to the bottom of it. So please forgive the prosecutor's seeming disrespect for the dead at this juncture. It is also a known fact that most local pastors can be outdrawn by a dead corpse at a funeral. More people come out to turn over garbage cans at funerals than come out to hear us on the Lord's Day. Many of our local parishioners hope that even the dead can offer them more than we can as local pastors from that preaching stage. And that is the truth, Your Honor. Even the dead have more to offer hungry folk then most of us from the pulpit.

So this court should see why the prosecutor saw it necessary to bring the dead into this nasty affair. Please forgive me. For when our folks look in such unseemingly places as funerals for a spiritual morsel, you can be sure that there is much spiritual fasting going on in our local churches all the time. Your Honor, and ladies and gentlemen of this jury, there is definitely a lenten season of spiritual fasting, going on 365 days a year, not every other day, but 365 days a year in most local churches with no spiritual food on this side of the Jordan for those hungry folks. And there is not even the hope of anything better on the other side of the Jordan River if what some of us proclaim about heaven is true, Your Honor. The way some jacklegs talk about heaven, they expect to have a jackleg on that preaching stage in heaven, Your Honor. The way they talk, it is going to be a funkmaker that is going to be sitting in the middle chair between those pearly gates. You are going to see a funkmaker up there in the middle chair. And then to top that off, every day, every day is supposed to be Sunday. You get the picture, with a jackleg running things on that heavenly stage with worship going on every day. Well, if that is the way that heaven is, Your Honor, and ladies and gentlemen of this jury, let me declare myself here and now, on this side of the Jordan about that situation. If heaven is going to be run by a funkmaking jackleg every day, then hell here I come, voluntarily. If heaven is like that, jacklegs running things every day, forever, then please Lord, remember me with the lost in hell, just reserve a place for me in hell.

Thus, Your Honor, and ladies and gentlemen of this jury, this court should now see clearly, I am not lying when I say that this sound is heard all over the land, BAM DE BAM BAM BAMA LAMA LAMA RING RING RING, all over creation now and supposedly in heaven later on, if heaven is like what those jacklegs are talking about.

Your Honor, and ladies and gentlemen of the jury, the prosecutor respectfully asks this court for a recess. We are not resting our case, not by a long shot, but we are merely calling for a recess in the trial, because we want to bring to this court expert witnesses who are now on the way by jet to testify for the prosecution against contemporary jacklegs. Your honor, and ladies and gentlemen of this jury, can I get this recess?

Recess granted.

5

The Sermonic Text

Sermonic text refers to identifying, distinguishing, and discriminating foundational ideas for our diversified preaching, by selecting a cohesive element from the Bible (99.44 percent of the time) or from some other source (.56 percent of the time), that will hold together every word, phrase, sentence, and paragraph into one body of communicative understanding for our hearers.

T HERE ARE TWO PARTS TO HOMILETICS, the homily and the rhetoric. We are now working on the homily, which involves the sermonic text. We are in the midst of defining what a sermonic text is by means of a sentence definition:

Text is that which flavors, pervades, or holds together an entity; in preaching, it is the genuine Word of God (frequently taken from the Bible) that flavors, pervades, or holds together the meaning of the sermon, so as to have divine sermonic communicative unity in our preaching.

There are three important elements involved in that definition:

1. A text in general is the foundational idea that makes any kind of discourse a sensible unit of meaning. You have got to have an underlying theme for any kind of writing or discourse if it is to make some sense. Even if you are talking about a cat, that cat is the text that is going to be underlying and woven through all what you are talking about in that cat presentation.

2. A preaching text in particular is different from other kinds of text in being exclusively restricted to the Word of God. A text makes a sermonic discourse a divine sensible unit of meaning. In a general text, you can talk about anything, but in preaching the

text has got to be on the Word of God. A text underlies, flavors, pervades, and holds together everything in a sermon.

3. The third clarification that we would make about that definition has to do with the parenthetical expression, namely, the words *frequently taken from the Bible*. We said that a text is that which flavors, pervades, or holds together an entity. In preaching, a text is the genuine Word of God (frequently taken from the Bible), remember that? Now why did I put those words in parentheses? Was I trying to assure you that I could be unique? And different? And significant? Is that why I used parentheses? Do you think that I wanted to put something in my definition to show you how to use parentheses? Certainly not!

The reason why I deliberately wrote that expression that way, in parentheses, was for deliberate teaching reasons. I do not want anybody at anytime to be misled by me into the fallacious notion that the Bible is the *only* resource for divine sermonic text. I don't want you to be fooled by that. So I deliberately wrote that expression in that peculiar way to protect myself from some biblical liars that go out from my class who might claim that I taught you that the Bible is the only source for the divine sermonic text in our preaching. Cause ain't no liar got no business telling lies on me about that now because of those parentheses.

Frequently, not all the time, the Bible is our source for sermonic text. Now let me say this. You must be sure that the Bible is the preeminent, chief resource for sermonic texts. So let me repeat that again, so that there will be no mistake about it in your minds. The Bible is the preeminent, chief resource for sermonic texts in our preaching.

In fact, 99.44 percent of the time you will have a biblical text for your preaching, which means that the Bible cannot be overlooked or minimized in your preaching nor in your theological education. That is why you start off with the Bible. If you don't know your Bible you can't do anything in ministry at all. You can't preach. You can't pray. You can't do no Christian education. You can't minister to no church. You can't counsel nobody if you don't have a fundamental understanding of the Bible in your theological education.

The Bible is also fundamental to your preaching. We are not minimizing the Bible—99.44 percent of the time you will be in the Bible, using the Bible as the textual base for your preaching. We get this figure from Ivory soap. In that ad for Ivory soap, they used to say—they don't say it anymore—that Ivory soap is 99 and 44 one-hundredths percent pure. Now, that is real pure, pure enough to be sitting on the water floating like an angel.

But, however, 99.44 percent is not 100 percent, even though we can say for all practical purposes it is 100 percent. If Ivory soap is 99.44 percent pure, then practically speaking it is absolutely pure. And that is what we are saying here. That for all practical purposes when we are talking about texts, we are talking about the Bible. I would not want to mislead, so I deliberately inserted that parenthetical expression in our working definition of "text." I deliberately wanted to remind you that a sermon can be homiletically sound without having a foundational text coming directly from the Bible. Are you folks hearing me? That is why you are learning about homiletical form; every text does not have to come from the Bible.

The real test as to whether one should use a suggested sermonic text, even from the Bible, must be based upon a theological judgment. The real test as to whether one will preach a given passage, even from the Bible, must be determined by whether that suggested biblical passage is indeed the genuine Word of God. It must be determined whether that suggested biblical passage was what our homeboy, Jesus, had in mind.

So using the Bible accurately or any other source for a text in our preaching involves theological expertise. That is why we require you to get some theology at this school. Theology is not an option but a requirement. You can't do nothing nowhere if you ain't theologically oriented. You can't preach because a homily is theology. And you certainly can't pray because you don't know how to reach God because you haven't studied the mind of God. And you certainly can't minister to nobody if you don't know what God has to say. How can you administer a church if you don't know what the ways of God are? How can you teach anybody if you don't know what God wants you to teach them? You got to have theological expertise!

For example, let me cite just one of many examples that could be cited as evidence of a biblical passage that could not be preached as the genuine Word of God on sound theological grounds. In Leviticus 24:20, we find "an eye for an eye and a tooth for a tooth," an expression that Jesus Christ, our homeboy expressly condemned as false doctrine. As a matter of fact, Jesus condemned a whole lot of stuff in the Old Testament that you need to know about. And some of you try to preach that stuff. Our homeboy told us that certain biblical passages can't be no homily, and if you preach that stuff then you are not in harmony with him. Leviticus 24:20 is one.

Jesus expressly condemned that Leviticus scripture in Matthew, where he said that you have heard it said of old, "an eye for an eye, and a tooth for a tooth," but I say to you that is false doctrine and you can't preach that no more. You have also heard that it has been said that you should love your friends and hate your enemies, but I say that is false doctrine and you can't preach that no more.

Jesus says that what he is telling us is that we ought to love our enemies. Say Amen to that. Do you hear me? When you start talking about Jesus as your homeboy, then Jesus says "Love your enemies." Look at Matthew. Read your Bible. Yes, Jesus said that, Love your enemy, because what good is it if you are just like the other people, who love only their friends?

So what we are saying is that Leviticus 20:24 is in the Bible, but you cannot preach that Leviticus passage as the genuine Word of God without calling Jesus Christ, our homeboy, a liar. So we condemn that particular passage from textual use on sound theological grounds although that spurious passage is in the Bible. Now, there are some resources other than the Bible from which we should and can get genuine sermonic texts from time to time.

So study the following suggestions on other appropriate resources for elaborating the Word of God as preaching texts. Christian hymns are commonly acceptable textual sources other than the Bible. There is nothing wrong with hymns as sermonic texts, except you don't want to preach on a Christian hymn without first making a theological judgment. Yes siree, you want to do that.

> In the Cross of Christ I glory;
> towering o'er the wrecks of time,
> all the light of sacred story
> gathers round its head sublime.

It ain't no pretty thing. No, it is not. It is ugly.

> When I survey the wondrous cross
> on which the Prince of Glory died
> my richest gain I count but loss
> and pour contempt on all my pride.

Preach that. That is what the cross is about. We ain't talking about preaching from other sources without a theological judgment. Most of the hymns are pretty good but check them all out theologically.

Church history is an acceptable source for sermonic texts. Christian biography—take people's lives as texts, if they are Christian, be sure that they are Christian now. Check it out before you use anyone's biography as a text. We even need to question the life of bishops for sermon material. Check them out theologically.

Elements of Christian rituals—ordination, sacraments, burials, marriage, traditional prayers, benediction, creeds—are all acceptable sources for sermonic texts. All of these are good. Check them out theologically because some of these texts are problem sources and need careful theological scrutiny. Classical literature, especially the writings of Shakespeare, may sound very theological but when you check it out, sometimes it is problematic, nothing but a do-do tale. Another example is the problematic verse "I am the captain of my ship, the master of my soul." I have heard that preached too many damn times. If you are the captain, then who is God? That is what it means to be converted. We say, I yield my will and my all to thee and God becomes the captain. Contemporary ballads can be used as texts in your preaching, but watch out for those popular songs. There is bad theology in a whole lot of them.

Let me indicate some of the times when it would be most appropriate to get the Word of God for our preaching texts from sources other than the Bible. There are times when we should leave that Bible alone and use other Christian resources deliberately. For instance, on Communion Sunday, it is most appropriate to get the textual word of God from the communion ritual itself, because there is genuine, living, divine truth in that communion ritual that needs to be expounded upon so that we can all participate in that holy sacrament more meaningfully. The way we fool around that communion table now is often a disgrace, pure disgrace, with no meaning in it at all. We just up there dogging down crackers and gulping down juice. That is why we desperately need to hear about the meaning of holy communion in a clarifying and sanctifying way many times from that pulpit. Folks ain't going to quit acting like a fool around that table if we don't clarify what communion is. That is why you don't preach a full sermon on Communion Sunday. If you do, you are just killing yourself for nothing.

Instead, you take an issue out of that communion ritual, "Ye that do truly and earnestly repent . . ." That is from the Bible, ain't it? It is talking about the nature, purpose, and calling of communion. Now, you are going to discuss that one point. You are going to *define* what you mean by "Ye, that do truly and earnestly repent." You are going to *elaborate* that. You are going to *exemplify* that. And you are going to *justify* the communion ritual. So that when members of the congregation come up there, and when you say that the next time, "Ye who do truly and earnestly repent," with that meaning behind them, then they know who you are calling. And some of the people who don't come to the communion table because they had misconceptions about it, they can come, and those who are up there who have misconceptions about it can now sit back in their seats. You take a meditation on Communion Sunday, every time you have communion, and after a couple or three years, folks will come up to the communion table and act like they got some sense.

The same thing needs to be done in reference to baptism. You need to preach some clarifying words on the meaning of baptism. You need to get something out of that ritual of baptism for a sermon. And for God's sake, don't try to have communion and baptism on the same Sunday. It is just like trying to have two guest speakers and trying to honor them both, which you can't. One of them is going to leave insulted. You can't give yourself to both of those rituals at the same time. It doesn't make sense to try and preach a full sermon when you have about four hundred folks to commune and then turn around and baptize every baby in the community—making me miss the damn football game. So the same thing applies to baptism if you want the people to participate in it with meaning. Every time you baptize, do a meditation, and the baptism becomes the proclaimed Word of God in an act. Do the same thing with baptism as with communion, so you save yourself. Yes.

And before you baptize, you Baptists are pretty good so I won't talk to y'all. I'm going to talk to you Methodists. You bring the baby in there and you don't even know who the baby is, ain't never met the baby nor the parents, and you are going to take it to the water, talking about holy baptism, and you ain't even talked with those parents about baptism. And no matter how cute that baby is, baptism ain't cute, it is serious. I appreciate my pastor for one thing. One time, somebody brought a cute baby in to be baptized and the pastor would not do it. I appreciate that. You must talk with the parents first about the meaning of that sacrament before you get up there. The parents need to be clear about what you are about to ask them to do in this ritual and if you don't make it clear, then you don't need to be up there. We will have no playing with the sacraments.

And God Almighty knows, we desperately need to hear some divine truth from that marriage ritual. Some of us in the church who have been married for years act as if we have completely forgotten or never heard tell of the meaning of our marriage vows made before God and the congregation at the altar. It is already a joke in terms of the lack of meaning that is there in so many marriages. Many of you desperately need to preach some relevant sermons on marriage or the marital disease will get worse and the strain will abound in our home life. And let me tell you this, there is nothing more that can hurt your soul, more than the problems at home. Nothing can hurt you more. You folks who are married need to be saying "Amen." And if you don't know about the hurt at home, it is because you have never been married; you are just living in the same house with another person and ducking each other. If you are married then you know that the deepest hurt you can get anywhere is at home. And so many church folks have never even heard what the will of God is in their marriage.

There are many jacklegs that are in business who will join even a dog and a cat together in a wedding ceremony and pronounce the benediction on that dog-and-cat wedding if the right amount of cash is passed by the groom. All you got to do is walk in there with your wallet hanging out of your pocket and jacklegs will do anything that you ask them to do. They will even do a dog-and-cat wedding, putting a dog and cat together, if the right amount of cash is flashed. That is why we have so many broken homes today, and so many children living without parents, because people are going to preachers who even put dogs and cats together. Other times, people come in drunk, maybe they just met, and they come to the preacher and he sees that wad of money hanging out of the man's pocket, and both the man and woman are staggering in there talking about we want to get married. So-and-so come in here and be a witness. No questions, no questions asked. No sense of honor. They don't even know each other and they are drunk, and we say, "What God has joined together; let no man put asunder." It isn't of God that we are speaking; it is the money.

So what we are indicating by that parenthetical expression in that textual definition is that the Word of God is divine truth, no matter where that divine truth comes from. It is safe to say that we are divinely obligated to preach all of God's divine truth in the Bible and outside the Bible whenever the human situation calls for a relevant truth being declared in the name of our Lord. Now to be sure, to be very sure, every text that we choose must be biblically inspired as well as biblically related, because our preaching must be related to the spirit of the Scripture even though we might not find in the Bible the same identical words as in our nonbiblical texts that we use from time to time.

For instance, I don't know if you will find the same identical words that are in the communion service or in the baptismal ritual expressed exactly the same way in the Bible. And yet I am convinced, without a doubt, that the sacramental rituals are definitely biblically related and biblically inspired. We need to preach those nonbiblical texts for the edification of a people, fully knowing that everything, all of God's Word, is not in the Bible.

Thus, in summary, we have said three things regarding the definition of a text: (1) that a text, in general, is the foundational idea that makes any discourse a sensible unit of meaning; (2) that a preaching text is different from other kinds of texts, in that a sermonic text is exclusively restricted to the Word of God in order to make a defined, sensible unity in our preaching; and (3) that the Bible is the preeminent resource for preaching texts, but not the only resource from which to get the Word of God for preaching in the name of the Lord.

6

Creative Textual Selections

Creative textual selections refer to theological considerations in choosing foundational ideas for preaching that are rich enough to support an entire sermon in terms of all the relevant questions that can be raised and heavenly answers needed by the human situation, since the foundational idea must be comprehensive enough to hold together the entire sermon, so that it is a real help for people desperately needing salvation.

OUR NEXT QUESTION is how to go about making creative judgments as to whether a suggested text is worthy of being preached or not. Anybody with an ounce of sense—and if you don't have an ounce then you know that I am not talking to you—knows that every idea that pops up in a preacher's head is not necessarily of God. Even our homeboy Jesus Christ had to do some critical judging in regard to the ideas popping up in his head out there in the wilderness, where he was tempted by the devil during those forty days. Ideas were popping in Jesus' head, that Jesus had to deal with. If there were ideas popping up in Jesus' head that he had to deal with, then you know the kinds of ideas popping up in your heads that you got to deal with.

Out there in the wilderness, even our Lord Jesus Christ, the Holy One of Israel, was taken to a high mountain by the devil himself, and the devil said, "Look out there! See what you can see. All that out there can be yours—fame, money, and all the loving you want. All that can be yours, and all you got to do to get it, it doesn't take much, you don't have to bow down to the ground, just flex a little." Now, don't get confused by the devil saying, "just flex a little," because when the devil says flex a little, the time will come when the devil says get your ass down on the ground and drag.

Now, what does that mean in terms of the black experience? What does it mean in terms of preaching? Now, what it could mean is this—what the devil wants you to do is flex just a little bit because you have too much intelligence and too much integrity, but for those other fools out there, the devil makes them get all the way down. And Jesus said to the devil, "Get thee behind me, Satan."

One of the things that the devil really wants you to believe is that the devil is working in everybody's best interests. Don't ever become so sophisticated that you don't believe that the devil exists, because the devil can do away with your congregation without you even knowing that he is there. What the devil likes for you to think about when you think about a devil is someone with horns and a tail, and you will not know that he is around until he gets you. Those pictures of the devil that you see are so obvious that it eventually makes you think that such a devil doesn't even exist. But I am telling you how the devil works now. The devil is ever busy trying to get preachers to hop on fallacies to feed to God's flock. That's what the devil works with—fallacies. The devil has always got some kind of fallacious lie coming around that seems like it is just what the doctor ordered from heaven—just like those mansions, money, booty, and everything else. And you ain't got to do much to get it. The devil says you can get your point across and he can get just a little bit of his. In reality, the devil gets all of his point across. We need to be forever on the alert against fallacious texts, some of which come directly from the Bible looking as beautiful as that wormy-gourmet apple in the Garden of Eden.

The devil can quote Scriptures because the devil knows Scriptures. The devil even quoted Scriptures to Jesus. The devil says, "I'll tell you what you can do to prove that you are the Son of God. Get your butt up on this high mountain and jump down, and if you don't get killed, then you are the Son of God. The Scriptures say that God will bear thee up, lest thou dice thou foot against a stone." That statement comes right out of the Bible. So the devil is using the Bible to make his point.

The devil uses the Bible in preaching too. The devil is ever busy concocting fallacies for preachers. Thus, you cannot march your bumkums up into that pulpit and preach every textual suggestion that you come across without checking it out first theologically, even those ideas you get from the Bible. Creating attractive fallacies in the preacher's mind so as to lead God's people astray is the devil's best trick. It has been the devil's most successful trick in human history—getting a whole gang of fools at one time by fooling the leader with a mind-fooling fallacy first.

If the devil can get the preacher, and then you get up in the pulpit with the people down there in the pews in faith looking at you with their mouths open, and the devil can get that preacher with that nasty collar on backwards, up there preaching, with that fallacy in mind, with all those homiletical skills, you will end up preaching the stuff of the devil, so as to get a whole congregation away from God at one time. The devil ain't got to work on everyone in the group, just fool the leader. Use the leader and the whole gang is the devil's. That is the devil's best trick in catching suckers by the carload, through preachers preaching fallacies on that stage. The devil gets a bumper crop every Sunday like that, in church. The devil gets more folks out of church then the devil gets off the streets in the ghetto and out of suburbia. The devil can get most of his converts by working right there in the pulpit. The devil doesn't want that one-at-a-time stuff. The devil bets on preachers like you, with nasty collars turned around backwards, who have been sent to the seminary to learn this rhetoric that you then put to a fallacy, putting the whole congregation in hell, easily.

Just because you sit at home and read the Bible does not mean that you are not in jeopardy. The devil can get to you. And if the devil gets to you before you sit down, then the devil knows that he has got you, because everything you read will look good to you. You can't get holy by dropping your butt down in a chair and saying, I am going to be holy for ten minutes—not with the devil on your shoulder, inside your head, creating attractive fallacies inside your mind to lead God's people astray. This is the devil's best trick. The devil gets more people out of church congregations than off the corner. That has been the devil's most successful trick in human history, getting a whole gang of fools at one time by fooling the leader with those fallacies to mislead your parishioners.

And whether you know it or not, people are sitting there in the pews hearing you with faith. Do you know that? That is why you need your ass kicked if you fool them. When they see a backwards collar, the people need to know that you are going to dialogue with them in honesty and truth. That's what wearing that collar means. And when you trick them, you need to be run out of town. I cannot love a black preacher who fools the people. The people have been hurt enough. They don't need to be hurt anymore. That is what the devil does. He gets a whole group in church by fooling the leader because the congregation is sitting up there following-the-leader, in faith. The devil ain't got to work on everyone in the group, just fool the leader and the whole gang is yours. Therefore, you need to learn some preliminary tests against fallacies at the foundation of your preaching. You need to learn how to do some truth testing at the text level of your sermonic endeavor.

For instance, your so-called best friend gives you a piece of meat—that would be nice in these times of inflation. And somehow your best friend comes up and says, "I got some meat for you." Thank you, Jesus, for you know how scarce things are, especially meat. But suppose you can smell that meat stinking through the wrapper when your friend hands it to you, smelling like a sack of do-do. "It is some meat here buddy. I know you are going through some hard times so I got some meat here for you." And that meat is stinking like a sack of manure. And suppose when you open up that wrapper you can see bits of green on that meat all the way to the bone—smelling like do-do, stinking real bad, and colored green through and through. I know the meat is a freebie and it is from your so-called best friend, and that means that it should be good meat. But if you can smell it stinking through the wrapper with your own nose, and you can see bits of green on it all the way to the bone with your own eyes, then why in the devil would you be looking up a recipe for cooking that rotting, stinking, green meat, even if it is free and from your so-called best friend? Now you don't need no expert vision, nor no expert chef, to find out whether or not your so-called best friend has played a low-down dirty trick on you with that rotten, stinking green meat in that package. You can check that nasty situation out all by yourself without an expert butcher, by means of a preliminary amateur test with your own nose and your own eyes. You will also know for a fact that something is radically wrong with the relationship with that so-called best friend of yours.

You call that fool a friend and there he is trying to poison you, giving you some cheap rotten meat that he found somewhere in a garbage can. How can you still call that rat your so-called best friend? All I can say is "ashes to ashes and dust to dust," and get ready to throw that silly ass in those weeds for being such a fool. To the Father, the Son and the Holy Spirit, whoosh!!! You can't kill yourself digging a hole to put your so-called friend in the ground. The dead ain't suppose to kill the living. It is just that simple. Throw his ass in the weeds because you should know from a preliminary amateur test—you don't need a professional—you should know from your own nose and your own eyes that something has gone awry in your relationship with that fool. Either that, or that fool show enough has a low estimate of your intelligence, thinking that you are crazy enough to cook up and to dog down in your belly some obviously rotten, stinking green meat like that. Something is wrong with your relationship with that so-called friend.

Even so, we are saying that when a suggested textual idea comes to you, even from your best friend, the Bible, you should give it some preliminary tests to see if it is stinking or has bits of green on it, before looking up the exegetical recipe for cooking it, and certainly before setting the homiletical table for serving it to the folk. You ain't got no business serving rotten textual meat to God's people since it always means a sure case of spiritual ptomaine poisoning coming directly from your preaching. And you ain't got no business calling yourselves no friend to humankind if you pull a low-down dirty trick like that on the people from the pulpit, either. Poisoning folk with textual meat and then calling yourself their best friend! That is what they eat, the Word, isn't it? And that meat is stinking and rotten. You can't be a friend to folk and feed them poison. Test that stuff and see if it is rotten and stinking and has bits of green on it before you serve it to God's holy people.

Thus, we may need to be reminded of what Saint Paul had to say about being suckers for fallacies. St. Paul talked about this. St. Paul said ages ago, "Test the spirit," meaning for us to check out every textual inspiration before trying to preach it on that stage. What we need to do is to make some acid tests at this crucial juncture of our preaching at the textual level. And thus, we have set up three preliminary acid tests. Hear me now, for this is a promise, for if you internalize these three acid textual testers that we are going to talk about, then you will not have to run around checking with biblical experts. If you learn what we are talking about concerning these three testers, you will be able to do this stuff yourself. And you are going to have to be able to test texts theologically yourself, because all of those seminary experts ain't going to be around and you will have to be the expert to make these preliminary tests in your preaching.

So, next time let us begin to look at those three testers in the name of the Lord, so that you can see if your sermonic textual meat is rotten, if it is stinking with bits of green on it, even as amateur preachers, because all those biblical experts here in the seminary ain't going to be around to help you out there in the preaching field.

7

Three Textual Testers

Three textual testers are the criteria or standards for selecting a foundational idea for undergirding a gospel proclamation based on (1) contemporary relevance, (2) genuine Word of God, and (3) completeness of thought. The foundational idea communicates who God is, how God operates, and God's will for us in meaningful idioms and thought patterns of the congregation, so that as preachers we can make creative judgments on the rightness or wrongness of our efforts at any given time in our sermonizing.

I F SERMONIC TEXTS ARE ESSENTIAL to your preaching, and if you will be preaching for the next forty to fifty years, then you need to figure out some way to get your hands on all those sermonic texts you are going to need in your preaching lifetime. So let me raise this question to get us started. Why is it necessary for us to go back to the past to pick up a text for a sermon to preach to people today? What does the past have to offer for the present needs in our preaching? The reason why a sermonic text is necessary has to do with what I call authoritative necessity, which is the practical need for our hearers to have the assurance that our preaching is of God for their ultimate response to our message.

Genuine preaching is always concerned about ultimate response to our God, always calling for an ultimate commitment of all of us to our God, always driving at getting a response of our body, mind, and soul. So our hearers must be put into position to be assured that what we are proclaiming for this ultimate response is of God, that is, if we expect for them to do more than merely knock them benches over in some kind of religious funk. No one should commit themselves ultimately to anything other than God almighty. God alone deserves our ultimate commitment and no one else.

So here we can begin to see that having an acceptable holy text at the very beginning of our proclamation has the practical value of assuring our listeners that our message is of God. A holy text from the hallowed past is of special value if that foundational text is from the commonly accepted Bible or from other commonly accepted sources for their ultimate response to the message. Wise preachers help their hearers to have the divine assurance by relating the sermonic discourse to a commonly accepted source of divine truth from the past at the outset. More than likely, we should relate the sermonic message to a biblical passage, or to an accepted statement in the holy sacramental ritual, or to a commonly accepted hymn, or to the commonly accepted creed, or to something else commonly revered and accepted from the past at the outset of the sermon for the congregation's ultimate response to our God.

Even jacklegs know that they need to have a text in order to gain people's assurance for hopping them on those benches with some slop for some cash. Even jacklegs know that they need to fool those hopping folks, by means of a commonly revered and commonly accepted source of divine proof from the past in order to attract them to that unholy slop that they plan to use in order for folks to jump those benches for some cash later on. Even jacklegs know that. So we need to be at least as wise as jacklegs, regarding the divine assuring business at the outset of our speaking, if we expect our hearers to make ultimate commitments by means of our preaching.

Now, this issue of being wise enough to assure one's hearers that this message is of God is often crucial in some preaching situations. It is often a matter of life and death in some denominations, like Methodist denominations. Many congregations are comfortably meeting new pastors just about every time that they look up into that pulpit. Every time they turn around a new stranger with a nasty collar on backwards is declaring, "I IS YOUR PASTOR, NOW! The bishop done appointed me here on yesterday. I is now your official pastor, at least for a day." And because there are so

many jacklegs on the prowl creating suspicion, people need some
kind of divine identification badges to allay their fears about all
those strange jacklegs taking over that pulpit, trying to get their
response. Just got a new pastor last week and now he's gone. Now
here's this strange, young, new whipper-snapper up in the pulpit
trying to get their response.

And there is no need for you Baptists and Presbyterians to
snicker, neither. At least we Methodists got one good thing, and
that is that the bishop will soon move trash away from there. You
Presbyterians and Baptists get stuck, so y'all ain't got nothing to be
snickering about. We can move new trash, whereas you Baptists
and Presbyterians have to keep that old trash.

Now, Peter and Paul, Luther and Wesley, the Bible and the
creeds—those Methodists all know and trust—but they do not
know and trust all those have-no-degree-traveling pastors that are
seeking their response. Those Methodist congregations have a
right to demand some kind of holy I.D. card from strangers with
nasty collars on backwards who are always popping up in
Methodist pulpits unannounced, trying to get a response to what
they are talking about. The congregation needs to know that you
are at least trying to relate to something of God, as soon as you get
your strange buncom-buncom up into that pulpit, because, after
all, they are only human.

Again, this issue of being wise enough to assure one's hearers
that your message is of God for a response is often crucial to
preachers in certain age brackets, especially if that preacher is
young and has bushy, nappy hair on his head and has not shaved
his face for a long time. Whether rightly or wrongly, we are not
debating the rightness or wrongness of it. Most church folks are
scared to death of young monkeys climbing their buncom-
buncoms up into the pulpit looking like that. You ain't got nothing to do but get your butt up there looking like that, with your
young crazy self and you have caused pandemonium in that place
for most church folks, even if you are of God.

Most conservative church folk are scared to death of young
folks, especially if you look like young radicals and hippies. You
try to get a response, but your voice, your being, and your appearance are scaring the congregation half to death. I am not saying

that it is wrong or right, but I am saying that there is fear when they see you coming up there like that, with all that bushy hair y'all got out there. You talk about you ain't going to shave. But, you young whipper-snappers do not have to look like a radical or a hippy to scare the daylight out of church folks. Most people in the *cullud* church are scared of young preachers who come from the seminary with all those newfangled ideas in your heads, even if you look as conservative as Little Lord Fauntleroy. There are a whole lot of *cullud* folks who still think that education ruins preachers anyway, especially if you take a course in homiletics. They still think that theological training takes away the spirit and prayer from preachers' lives and from your ability to preach with power.

The Bible they know and trust, but you young whipper-snappers they definitely do not know and do not trust, and they are usually scared to death of you. You young whipper-snappers definitely need the aid of some commonly accepted holy authoritative texts to help assure them about you for their ultimate response. The congregation does not want you up there tampering with God's word with your young radical ideas from the seminary. Now, whether they realize it or not, the Bible is far more radical than you young whipper-snappers will ever be. The Bible is far more radically concerned to call them to repentance and to take up a cross. Whether those conservative folks realize it or not, most of you young whipper-snappers are far more interested in giving them merely a verbal treat for a jumping response for some cash later on.

But there is one big difference between you and the Bible, namely, that the congregation will more readily accept a radical idea if that radical idea can be proved to be scripturally based. Even though radical at points, they believe that the Bible is of God for their ultimate response. And we do need radical preaching, not conservative preaching, radical preaching, getting at the roots of things that we are talking about here, not smoothing over the surface. We are not giving people skin operations but we are giving them operations for cancer deep inside their souls. We are concerned about radical preaching, so that people can be radically changed to live in radical obedience to our radical God. All of our preaching definitely needs the assurance of the radical but accepted authority of the ages for men and women to respond ultimately. You definitely need radical foundational texts from the radical Bible or from the radical creeds or from the radical sacraments or from the radical hymnody, or from other radical Christian sources that have stood the test of time and thus have become hallowed by the ages for the congregation's natural ultimate response to them.

We are not talking about really going back to something old in the past just because we want to impede future progress. But rather, what we are talking about is that future progress is necessarily dependent on the tried and true of the past. Because there are some things tried and true and accepted from the past, we need to ground our sermons on those solid textual foundations in our past. We expect people to believe that what we proclaim is of God for their ultimate response to our God. Well now, did I justify that point? If so, now go and do thou likewise in your preaching.

Now, if you learn the following three textual testers, you can figure out sermonic texts for yourself. The first tester is what I call *contemporary relevance*. Contemporary relevance is something of vital significance to the needs and problems of the audience, since people are the end and goal of our preaching. This first test should remind us of the part of our working definition of preaching that is concerned with contemporary issues. This first tester focuses on making a judgment as to whether or not the text has vital, living significance for the needs and problems and sins and aspirations of the particular people to whom a particular sermon will be delivered.

In other words, you do not choose a text merely because you *laks* it, nor just because it looks good and you *laks* it. That is not the reason you select a text to preach. You select a text in the light of women and men's needs, not because you *laks* it and it sounds pretty to your ears. The text is never selected because it is a pretty biblical passage that tickles our aesthetic sensibility. Primarily you choose a sermonic text because it will be helpful in some vital ways to the people hearing it.

Now, I am fully aware that this principle of relevant judgment runs counter to some minds because some of you are accustomed to preaching the same sermon in different places, especially if that same sermon is your so-called famous sermon. Hell! How are you going to have a famous sermon if you ain't famous yourself? Others of you ride that so-called famous textual horse in order to make a big hit in your preaching, especially when you go guest preaching in big churches in Atlanta, Montgomery, and Memphis. "Make sure you use that pile of manure." And you don't even realize that your so-called famous sermonic text ain't nothing but a pile of manure.

So, all too frequently without regard for different social, economic, political, educational, and religious conditions of different congregations in different circumstances—all too frequently, some of you go to that same old textual stable to try to ride that same old broken-down irrelevant mare, and try to make you a general message for all sorts and conditions of *menses* and *womenses* when we have an outside engagement and sometimes when we have an inside engagement. It is possible that you have done this in good conscience up to now. Those were days of ignorance. But let me proclaim to you this day that such irrelevant hash slinging and such irrelevant generalizing is a homiletical sin for you from this day forward. From now on, you do know better, for the mouth of the Lord has spoken it through this first principle of judgment and through this official proclaimer saying it to you now.

So let us be unmistakably clear about this. For when you decide on any sermon from any text that does not have your hearers particularly and specifically in mind, then you have deliberately transgressed the second commandment of God. You have violently sinned against the divine commandment to love your neighbor, by not considering your neighbor's real needs in your preaching. For the needs of people are far more significant in the sight of God than mere pretty ideas, even from the Bible. And only when your textual ideas are grounded upon the final interests—I don't mean human interests but the final interests—of the people addressed are they holy ideas with divine duty. Even if they are so-called biblical pretty ideas, they are still ugly if they are not relevant to your congregation.

Even biblical texts cannot be judged to be holy and beautiful unless they are relevant for the people hearing us talk about them. Even the Bible itself expresses support for this issue of relevance in selecting holy beautiful texts for your preaching. For example, the

Hebrew writer puts it well when he says that the holy message of God that was delivered in the being of Jesus Christ was not for angels in heaven to be dancing on but for men and women who need it for salvation.

Again, for example, our homeboy Jesus Christ would say that texts, even biblical texts, were made for men and women and not men and women for pretty texts. Even the Bible itself expressly suggests a higher judgment than the Bible for testing the validity even of biblical texts for your preaching. The Bible itself suggests that the religious welfare of men and women be a basic criterion for your preaching always. For this is the only kind of neighborly love that is really significant in your preaching, sharing with your neighbor some good textual meat that can be used, rather than some rotten textual meat that needs to be in a garbage can somewhere even though we think it's pretty.

In a word, whenever you have a preaching engagement anywhere, whether as a pastor or a guest preacher, whenever you have a preaching engagement anywhere, you are to capture a vision of the multitude first, just as our homeboy did in seeing the multitude and its needs on that mountain. Only after you have really envisioned the needs of men and women should you open your mouth to teach them, and teach them with a loving relevant text, just like our homeboy did on that mountain ages ago.

Thus, *contemporary relevance* is the psychological and sociological bearing of a divine idea on life. It is one judgmental principle that must be at the root of a sermonic text as a foundational text. This judgment is crucial for accepting or rejecting, for a preacher saying "I Will" or "I Won't" accept a suggested text that dawns upon you for preaching to the desperate needs of people around you in holy relevant love. Now, you got that—*What* we are talking about? *How* we are talking about it? and *Why* we are talking about it?

Now, the second tester is what I call *genuine Word of God*, something of authentic redemptive significance as opposed to the spurious and accidental. There is sand as well as gold in them hills. Genuineness. Now, this second test should remind us of the second part of our working definition of preaching, namely, the Word of God. Well, this second tester is concerned with making a judgment as to whether a suggested text has vital divine significance for helping people in depth.

The first principle is to make sure that we help the congregation, and here, in the second, we are talking about helping in depth the ills and ailments of the particular people to whom a particular sermon will be delivered. In other words, you do not choose a text merely because a gang of fools tells you that they like it. Neither is it selected merely on the basis of sociological, popular demand.

For instance, I remember a person on this staff coming to me after one of my class sessions, saying "I heard you preaching this morning. I hope you choose that text on Ezekiel and the Valley of Dry Bones sometimes, *cause chile* I enjoys that sermon." I responded to her in this manner, "Well I won't be taking that text in my class where I call myself teaching, not preaching. But if I ever do take that text I don't think that you will enjoy hearing me preach it." For we do not choose a text on the basis of popular, foolish demands from a gang of fools wanting to get their kicks. You do not get your textual inspiration from fools selecting it for you. Texts are selected for your congregation so that they can apply the sermon to overcome their sins.

So, whereas the first testing principle does give due consideration to the human situation, this second testing principle does not permit regard for human whims and fancies in selecting a text. In addition to the human factor, the second principle demands a consideration of the divine aspect of preaching texts, which means that your sermonic text must be theologically sound, critically based, religiously true. So ain't no monkey with a nasty collar on backwards got no business climbing his or her buncom-buncom up there in that pulpit based solely on popular demand from the folk. "Will you preach that one again? Hell, no! You should have got it the last time. Hell, no!"

Preaching by definition has to do primarily with a divine demand, with a divine text based upon the will and intent of our Maker for men, women, and children to live by, and not the will and intent of some fools who want to get their kicks. Preaching has to do primarily with religious salvation, having to do with our concern for edification and restoration of the people addressed with God's basic will and intent for their lives. Thus, individual texts must reflect the genuine Word of God at its source.

Now, let me clear up a point here about the relation of God's basic will and intent to the Bible. Unless one is perfectly naive or a biblical literalist or a nappy-headed fool, one can easily recognize even with a superficial inspection that not every biblical text is religiously celebratory and edifying and restoring for preaching. To be sure, we are aware that there is no limit to the gold in those biblical hills, no doubt about that, but, we should be aware that there is much sand in those biblical hills also. There ought to be no doubt about that either. Any competent miner always knows that there is more sand than gold in any gold mine. Even an incompetent miner knows that. And any competent miner also knows that all that glitters and is yellow is not necessarily gold. So many competent miners without much education know the distinctive difference between gold and sand in a gold mine. But sad to say, sad to say, many preacher miners, with and without education, don't often know the distinction between preaching gold and preaching sand as far as biblical gold mines are concerned. It is not uncommon to see many preaching miners picking up the biggest piece of biblical sand that they can find and trying to peddle it off from the pulpit as if it were genuine biblical gold. It happens time and time again from the pulpit every Sunday.

There are so many monkeys coming up and polishing off nothing but a big piece of biblical sand that doesn't mean nothing at all for salvation. I don't know whether it is because most preachers are lazy or because they are crazy. Either lazy or crazy is the popular explanation of it. But for some reason you find preachers frequently trying to peddle off from the pulpit nothing but some biblical sand as if it is biblical gold. That is exactly why I keep on saying that there ain't no young, nappy-headed preaching aspirant got no business trying to pick up no preaching lessons from most of those old nappy-headed jacklegs out there in the field. What most jacklegs can teach you is how to pick up a big piece of religious poop from the Bible and try to pelt it for religious truth, and religious poop can't save nobody, even if it is from the Bible.

Now, the reason why so many preachers with nasty collars on

backwards take their buncom-buncoms up there in the pulpit with nothing but some religious poop is more than likely a failure to make a logical judgment of suggested biblical texts. That is why you need to study your theology. When you start talking about I'm going to be a preacher, then you need to study your theology real hard, because you have got to make theological judgments on every text that you use. So many jacklegs run around on that biblical desert and often see religious mirages with biblical sand looking like it is biblical gold.

Now I have an example here of how some un-Christian biblical texts are used or abused by either lazy or crazy preachers who often try to peddle religious poop from the pulpit. This example has to do with my seminary days, when we had worship services at night three times a week conducted by the students in the seminary. We also had worship services twice a week in the daytime where the faculty members were in charge. And we would have some students doing the preaching, such as it was, and other students conducting the worship service, such as that was, also.

Well anyway, one time when I was scheduled to do the preaching, such as it was, it happened that a jackleg classmate of mine was scheduled to conduct the worship service with me. So before the service he asked me what Scripture I had in mind and I suggested that he read anything that he found appropriate. I did not have a particular Scripture as the basis for my *mess age*, because I did not believe in the Bible too much at that time anyway. I knew that that monkey was either lazy or crazy. I knew that about that fool with his eyes batting and bouncing all the time like somebody dribbling a basketball. I could tell by that fool's eyes that something was wrong with him but I did not know how bad off he was until that night when he picked up a big piece of biblical poop and tried to jump us monkeys with it in that service. I knew that he was way off from then on. He was not lazy. I knew that fool was just plain crazy.

Now, that monkey chose to read a portion of the first chapter of Matthew as the appropriate Scripture for us to feast our souls on. I guess he opened the Bible at random, and the first place that his batting eyes fell was suppose to be a revelation of the Holy Spirit from on high with appropriate power of salvation. Well, he read this for our devotional meditation from the Bible in that worship service. "Abraham begat Isaac. Isaac begat Jacob. Jacob begat Joseph. And Joseph begat . . . and begat begat begat. . . . And begat begat begat. . . and Joseph begat Jesus the Son of God."

And then that monkey had the audacity to say after that, "And may God add a blessing to the reading of his Holy Word." Now, what holy word was that? It is no more significant to me to hear about those begats in the Bible than to hear that old mangy Rover, the dog, begat Fido. What holy word was the Lord suppose to bless in reading that? For there is nothing religiously salutary about birth no matter whose it is. Only rebirth has significance for salvation. Yet somehow, to that fundamentalist classmate of mine and to some others, there is a need to prove that Jesus had blue blood in his veins. Good breeding by birth is not the weightier matter of the Christian religion.

Yet we are told by the Scriptures themselves that the Word that became flesh was not according to the will of the flesh. The Bible says that it is not of blood but according to the will of God. It ain't got nothing to do with the way of Jesus' birth but with the way of God in that birth. But this so-called Bible toting, Bible-thumping fundamentalist fool overlooked all that spiritual meaning in the Scriptures and tried to jump us monkeys with those irrelevant physical begats. And he did break up that service because the students in the pews were chuckling all during my *mess age.* I should have given the benediction rather than try to go on, because that fool had stolen the whole show that night. All I was doing up there was talking. And it is a fact that many preachers often grab a theological snack, rather than a theological steer, and try to prepare a spiritual meal out of a theological snack.

I feel the urgent need to drive home the idea that a suggested text for preaching must have some theological weight to it. A sermonic text must be more than a theological snack in order to feed a whole congregation of folk for salvation. Without theological weight in our sermonic text, one is merely involved in trying to make chicken salad out of chicken droppings. And the best chef in the world cannot make no nasty chicken droppings taste like no nice chicken salad, no matter who the chef is. No matter how much that chef knows, no matter what the chef puts in it, it is still going to taste like chicken droppings, no matter what happens to it.

Trying to whip up a nice spiritual meal out of a honky-donk text is going to taste like that do-do chicken salad no matter what happens to it. Because you certainly must have a text with some theological weight to it in order to satisfy that deepest hunger in men and women for salvation. And anything, anything of lesser theological significance has no value for preaching, just ain't worth nothing, even if a black angel from heaven says otherwise. It is still a lie even if it is a black angel from heaven. A sermonic text has got to have theological weight if it is going to have power for salvation.

The genuine Word of God, with the redemptive bearing of a divine idea on life for people's internal liberation, is a second judgmental principle that must be at the root of a sermon as its foundational text. This judgment is crucial for accepting or rejecting, for saying "I will" or "I won't." It is crucial for accepting or rejecting a text for preaching to the deepest theological needs of people around you for their salvation.

Now, the third and final acid test that we should give to every suggested biblical text that raps at the door of our preaching establishment, trying to engage our sermonic attention as we check out fallacious texts, is *completeness of thought*. Completeness of thought means that we choose a biblical text that is genuinely propositional in nature (as opposed to a mere word, phrase, or dependent clause), since a foundational idea for a sermon can only be ensconced in a sentence or paragraph or chapter or groups of the same. The prime example of violating the principle of *complete thought* is the way many people try to use parables as sermonic texts, without reference to the thesis that the parable is illustrating.

A lot of big preachers misuse the parable of the Prodigal Son to preach on Christ and the Christian family. The real meaning of the Prodigal Son deals with a time when Jesus was being criticized for consorting with unreligious folks. Jesus uses this parable to prove that God is concerned with sinners and saints alike. Two other parables, the Lost Sheep and the Lost Coin, are about this same thesis, God's universal love, and not about how to raise cattle nor

how to sweep up lost pennies. Parables are rinds and nutshells—
the thesis is the goodie!

Well, we have now covered the three acid tests that we should
give to every suggested text that raps at the door of our preaching
establishment trying to engage our preaching attention. Yes, you
need to use these three tests for checking out fallacious texts. And
if God wills, I will share with you the formal rhetorical elements
of a sermon the next time we meet in the Lord's name.

8

Sermonic Title, Introduction, and Proposition

Title, Introduction, and Proposition are three of the six formal elements in the construction of a sermon (the others are Text, Body, and Conclusion). This structure is based on our unique rhetorical obligations to use the most logical expressions for persuading, convincing, and edifying the judgment of our hearers, so that as preachers we understand how sermon designs are determined and comprehend why certain sermons take specific shapes.

L ET ME BEGIN BY SAYING that I have an interest in your prayers for me at this time. I have had some crises since I last saw you and I do have interests in your prayers. I am not going to seem at my best today because I need strength and power. I don't want to fool you. I can't fool you because you mean too much to me. But I do ask an interest in your prayers and your wisdom. When you really settle down, and you are thinking about the concerns of the day and people on your prayer list, then remember me when you pray. I want you to kind of help me out this morning. And if you have some thoughts that need prayer, then let us include them.

Are you ready? Come on, I got more than one person in this class. I already told you that I need your support this morning. Let's act like we are together. I need all your help. Sometime I can lead by myself but today, I need your help. Don't lag behind, now. Ready? Ready to go?

YES SIR!

SERMONIC TITLE
Name of It

The *sermonic title*, commonly designated the *subject*, names that which the specific sermon is about. The title/subject is an absolute necessity. The title/subject informs the congregation how to hear the particular vein of the unsearchable riches of Christ to which they should turn their thinking. In addition, the title/subject is necessary for sermonic integrity because it is brought in as a plumb line for each paragraph, illustration, point presented. And because the preacher will be bombarded with temptatious ideas both from the Devil and from the Spirit up to and including the time of delivery, a precise title/subject will help in making a judgment.

In accordance with two factors that I use in classifying *sermonic titles*, the word *title* is the more appropriate name for this, because the *title* names the subject with all of its modifiers. The first type of structural classification for the *title* involves two foundational parts of speech for formulating meaningful human expressions, namely, nouns and verbs, upon which all other parts of speech depend in meaningful human expressions.

A *substantial title* has to do with a type of sermonic naming that is composed primarily of a basic noun/pronoun (plural or singular) with its modifiers, designed to aim at either new thinking (mind, plural) or new being/decision (soul, singular)—as the ultimate response sought. The text of Matthew 16:24 ("If any man [or woman] would come after me, let him [or her] deny himself [herself], take up his [or her] cross, and follow me.") could have as an exemplary *substantial title* for the mind (thinking) "Steps Toward Personal Greatness," and for the soul (being) "Movement Toward Personal Greatness."

A *dynamic title* is a kind of sermonic naming that is composed primarily of a basic verbal (never a verb, but a verbal such as a gerund, an infinitive, or a participle, which are verb-words being used as nouns or adjectives) with its modifiers, designed to aim at new action/doing (heart) as the ultimate response sought. An exemplary *dynamic title* for the heart (action) could be "Moving Toward Personal Greatness."

The second classification of *sermonic title* is the subject matter: *thinking, deciding, acting*. The procedure for determining the subject-matter *title* involves being physicians of the soul. Diagnosis is where we observe the symptoms of spiritual ailments in our congregation, making us aware that a spiritual problem is there for relevant (relieving, reliving, resurrecting) sermonizing. Etiology is where we theologically research the cause of spiritual ailments in our congregation to determine why a spiritual problem is there, for relevant (relieving, reliving, resurrecting) sermonizing.

A *thinking title* is used when the cause of the spiritual ailment is ignorance. Then the design is with plural nouns, since the mind is illuminated in terms of analysis being suggested by plural nouns in each body point—"steps." Some appropriate thinking words to be ringing out throughout the whole sermon would be "idea," "comprehend," "meaning," "understand," "for your consideration," "for your attention," "knowledge," "wisdom," etc.

A *deciding title* is used when the cause of the spiritual ailment is lack of will-power/weakness. Then the design is with singular nouns, since the soul is disposed to wholeness, suggested by singular nouns—"movement." Either the whole hog or none. Deciding words would include "integrity," "authenticity," "being/non-being," "decision," "will," "choice," "resolution," "option," "confidence," etc.

An *acting title* is used when the cause for the spiritual ailment is helplessness/laziness. Then the design is with verbals (not verbs), since the heart is stimulated by means of activity, suggested by verbal nouns and adjectives. E-motion-al outreach is what the heart pants after. Examples of acting words are "doing something," "getting going," "moving out," "giving it a go," "getting off the rusty-dusty," "busying yourself," etc.

Suggestions for Constructing a Title/Subject

1. *Relation to text.* The meaning of the text should flavor, pervade, and hold together the sense of the subject.

2. *Variation from text.* While carrying the meaning of the text, the title should be expressed in different words; the subject is

the statement of the text "in other words," or is the text "coined" for the market.

3. *Relevance.* The title should bear words and meanings that are commonly understood by, and genuinely related to, the experience of lay theologians.

4. *Specificity.* Through the use of modifying words and phrases, the title should relate to some specific meaning of the unsearchable riches of the Word of God found in the text.

5. *Conciseness.* The title should embrace the meaning of the text and the specific idea of the sermon in five words or less.

Common Errors in Constructing Titles

1. *Fallacy of the universal.* You should not foolishly choose to title the sermon with such generalities as "GOD," "LOVE," "FAITH," "SALVATION," etc. without modifiers.

2. *Fallacy of the abstruse.* You should not attempt to impress the congregation with your learning by using technical jargon, for example, "The Implications of the Atonement for the Soteriological Undergirding of the Orders of Creation."

3. *Fallacy of the parrot.* A lazy individual repeats portions of the cited text, thinking that by using the same "holy" words in the title he/she is coining God's Word for public consumption. Really you are avoiding the task of making the whole sermon, including the title, interpretative.

4. *Fallacy of the unsemantic.* You should not foolishly use a subject and a predicate and call it a title, for example, "GOD CARES," "DOES GOD CARE?" "DO YOU KNOW HIM?" or "I NEVER KNEW HIS NAME."

5. *Fallacy of the sensationalistic.* You should not foolishly use striking expressions to attract people to the title rather than to the Word of God, for example, "SHAKE, RATTLE AND ROLL," "NOTHING BUT A HOUND DOG," "IF LOVING YOU IS WRONG."

Our sermonic naming is related to the ultimate command of God, in connection with loving God with all our mind and soul and heart, for leading people deliberately to be in harmony with our God by our proclaiming. In other words, these types of titles/subjects guarantee that the first and great commandment will be more and more fulfilled by people in the church, since these three types of titles/subjects are gearing toward loving our God with all our minds, our hearts, and our souls. Correct naming aids in correct aiming of our sermons all the time—substantially and dynamically.

SERMONIC INTRODUCTION
Reason for It

Now, in order to begin this rhetorical element right, let me begin this item by making an emphatic judgmental statement about the significance of the *sermonic introduction*, in relation to the other five items of homily-rhetoric—*text, title, proposition, body*, and *conclusion*—namely, that the *sermonic introduction* is not an essential element of the sermon in the same sense as the other five items are. Now, hear me well! I did not say that an introduction is not important to a sermon. I merely said that the *sermonic introduction* is *not essential* to a sermon in the same sense as the other five items of homily-rhetoric.

"Well, now! Looks *lak* Doc done tore his britches! Cause every textbook book on *homi-ca-letics* includes a section on sermonic introduction. So, how can Doc get away with saying that sermonic introductions are *not essential* to a sermon? Ole Doc done stuck his foot in his own *muf dis* time!!"

You must learn to distinguish essential from important. Many things can be important to us, and still not be essential to us, and we need to learn the difference. An introduction is like a banana peel—it gets the banana to us in safe condition—while the *text, title, proposition, body*, and *conclusion* are like the goodie—goodie of the banana per se for eating purposes.

For instance, on that awful night in Montgomery, Alabama, involving Rosa Parks, no introduction was necessary, since everybody there at the mass meeting knew *why* they were there that night, meaning that they could get on with the *proposition* (how to overcome).

Our judgment about the nonessentiality of introductions does not mean that they are unimportant. We need to know how to do a bang-up job on introductions 99.44 percent of the time, so we can get away from dishing up slop at the front of our *mess-ages* as the spiritual appetizer.

Thus, because sound introductions are important to our sermonizing 99.44 percent of the time, and because there is a desperate need for quality on this issue, homiletics authors (John Broadus and H. Grady Davis) and yours truly find it expedient to guide you in this important area of homily-rhetoric. A well-constructed, meaningful sermonic introduction does serve a stimulating, useful, wonder-working, morale-building, *important* function in leading people into the very heart of God's Word 99.44 percent of the time. So the crucial issue is not whether or not sermonic introductions are essential. But, rather, the crucial question is whether or not we are able to be workmen/workwomen who need not be ashamed in leading people into pastures green for reviving weary souls, leading people into the very heart of what our sermons are all about, in the name of our Lord. Amen! And, Amen!

Sermonic introduction is defined as the preliminary discussion by which the hearers are led meaningfully into the heart of the discourse. Picturesquely speaking—it is like a porch that leads into the inner chambers of a house. Symbolically speaking—it is like saying, "Mr. Doe, I would like to acquaint you with Ms. Brown." Each sets the stage for entering into serious engagement with, and deep dialoguing on, the more significant matters forthcoming in the essential discussion. All parts of this definition suggest that the introduction is not an essential part of preaching per se, though it is an important part—since it is not really the Word of God, but is merely the spiritual ailment.

The first part of this definition—that the introduction is *preliminary* and *leads into*—implies that the introduction is not the main attraction, not the heart itself. The second part of the definition—that the introduction is *like a porch*—implies that it is not the place where folks live out their lives. The third part—that the introduction is *like a personal introduction*—implies that the introduction is not what the man and woman will talk about later on. And the last part, *setting the stage,* implies that the introduction is not the real drama to be played. Literally, *intro* means "into" or "inside" (not "between," as the term *inter* would mean); and *duct* means a "pipe" or "lead" or "entrance."

Attention-Attracting Principle

The *attention-attracting principle* is the "why" and "how" of introductions. Sermonic introductions are a means of capturing the awareness of our hearers in that preliminary discussion through stimulating, motivating first sentence(s) at the beginning of the preliminary discussion. The introduction should inspire the hearers to want to listen to the rest of the sermon. (To make their ears stand up like Bugs Bunny's.) For example, the Drill Sergeant says to his Beetle Baileys and Gomer Pyles: "Companeh, Atten—tion!!!" Those Beetle Baileys and Gomer Pyles can be found out there in our audiences in church desperately needing to hear us say, "Companeh, Divine Atten—tion!!!"

One factor in the attention-attracting principle is the creative first sentence. We need to produce extraordinary and striking first sentences, by means of rump/knee work and hard thinking in the preaching workshop by our lonesome self with the Lord. Another factor in this principle is the psychological first sentence. We need to have something peculiarly interesting for them in that first sentence—such as some kind of salmon for those cats, or some kind of No-doz for those sleepers. (Not a Bible roll call of the saints of old, Abraham, Sarah, Hagar, Isaac, Rebekah, Esau, Jacob, Moses, Joshua, Peter, Mary, Martha, Paul, or even Jesus.)

Examples of mind-killers: "Jesus Christ is real nice, ain't he, folks?" (pure Sominex). "God the Father who sent us J-e-e-e-e-s-u-s sho nuff is real nice" (more sleeping pills). The Holy S-p-i-r-i-t sho nuff warms you up inside real nice; don't it folks?" (an overdose of sleeping pills).

Examples of mind-stimulators: The beginning of this discussion, setting up an argument with you on introductions not being essential. (Companeh Atten—tion!!!!) My Introduction in a Minister's Institute: "Today, we have come to wrestle with an issue which I believe separates the men from the boys, and the women from the girls, as professionals or experts in communicating the gospel effectively—namely, the issue of procedures in relevant gospel proclamation." (Companeh Atten—tion!!!!) Question stimulators: "What could really make us or break us in our preaching? What do we really need to know that could turn the tide for us in our preaching? Today we have come to . . ." Good questions always draw attention. (Companeh Atten—tion!!!!)

Problem-Raising Principle

The *problem-raising principle* is a second "why" and "how" of introductions. The problem-raising nature of the *sermonic introduction* means that we are concerned to have a psychological stimulus as the preliminary discussion to show *what, how,* and *why* our hearers are seriously and ultimately involved with the divine issue under discussion, so that they can really have a personal, ultimate concern for hearing the sermon the rest of the way.

One of the rationales for problem raising has to do with the insensitivity of most people in general about their spiritual condition. Often they must be sensitized to their spiritual illness, if we expect them to take spiritual medicine in sermons. The insensitivity of church folk about their spiritual condition is due to self-deception about their church participation. Church folk often must become aware that they are heading for a spiritual grave if we expect them to be interested in doing more than merely hopping the *bainches* on gospel medicine in sermons.

The *how* of problem raising has to do with logical procedure for designing the whole sermon all the time, in terms of establishing a logical connection between the meaning of the sermonic introduction and the meaning of the rest of the sermonic discussion forthcoming all the time, so that what we *begin with* is seen to have a direct bearing on what we *continue with* and *end with* all the time, namely, a problem being faced tied to an answer from God on it, or a human question tied to a divine answer.

An example of the *how* of problem raising is found in the medical profession. Diagnosis is the first process for understanding the

SERMONIC TITLE, INTRODUCTION, AND PROPOSITION   103

nature and cause of the ailment—similar to the nature of the *sermonic introduction*. The prescription is the second process for curing the diagnosed ailment, similar to the *sermonic body* and the *sermonic conclusion*.

Another example of the *how* of problem raising is a personal experience. One day in May of 1964, the doctor diagnosed me with diabetes. He told me "what I had," "how I had it," and "why it could kill me!!" His prescription advised me to watch my diet, to keep in touch with him, and to buy a book on the subject to be informed. My reaction was that I started counting calories like King Midas counting his money; I got that recommended book well marked up; and I carry his telephone number on me everywhere I go. I heard every last word the doctor said that day.

With problem-raising introductions we must indicate the nature (*what*) of the problem, the manifested location *(how)* of the problem, and the consequences left to us, the reasons *(why)* the problem is serious—choosing catastrophes under the devil or blessings under God.

Suggestions for Constructing a Sermonic Introduction

1. *Relational identity.* The introduction is not a point of the sermon per se; it does a job for the sermon, but it is not an immediate member of the family.

2. *Singleness of thought.* The introduction does only one job in introducing the sermon. The one sermonic porch may be elaborate, but it is still one porch. We need only one porch to a house, not two front porches.

3. *Uniqueness.* Each sermon should have its own, particular unique introduction. If an introduction can fit two sermons, it is probably good for neither.

4. *Brevity and Proportion.* The introduction should be one-tenth to one-fifth of the sermon. This depends on the nature of the subject matter. Some sermons are hard for the congregation to know, while others are easy for them to know.

5. *The "Alpha."* The first sentence of the introduction should be the "second" best in the entire sermon, "second" only to

the last sentence in the conclusion. All should be sentences, but these two should be the two pearls of great price.

6. *Question-raising.* Raise these kinds of questions in deciding upon the introduction:

- What kind of introduction must and will prepare my hearers to receive this sermon?

- What is the most striking way (not sensationalistic) I can express this introduction in my first sentence?

- How foreign is this subject to my hearers, which indicates how much introducing will be needed?

7. *Temporal inferiority.* The introduction should not and cannot be written before the *proposition* is precisely stated, since the introduction is to serve the particular demands of the sermon. In fact, it might be a wise principle to write introductions last always. We ought to know what we are trying to introduce.

Types of Introductions

1. *Textual.* Give significant data or information about the text, if the textual message looms as the most difficult item needing clarification.

2. *Subjective.* Clarify the significance of or reasons for selecting the subject of the discourse, if a problem looms here.

3. *Occasional.* Express the meaning or history of the occasion at hand, if the occasion is special. Don't overlook communion and baptismal occasions.

4. *Experiential.* Narrate a problem encountered by you and/or others, if such is germane to the issue at hand.

5. *Parable.* Put the issue into a living context, so that people can see its meaning in a dynamic picture.

6. *Question-raising.* Inspire interest by raising ultimate questions about the issue at hand. "What shall I render unto the Lord, my God, for all His benefits unto me?"

7. *Communal experience.* Begin with a shared experience known by all, and proceed to the new truth.

8. *Relative anecdote.* Share a humorous statement that has bearing on the issue. Be careful and prudent here.

9. *Quotations.* Use literary gems that express most accurately what you might say in introducing the sermon.

10. *Infinite variety of other sources.* Whatever combination of types listed above or whatever method you employ, be sure that the introduction is the servant to the sermon, never the master.

Common Errors in Introducing Sermons

1. *Fallacy of pity me*—where one begins with excuses about personal ailments or about lack of time for preparation because of a busy schedule. The quickest way to kill interest is to tell people not to expect anything worthy of their attention. If you are too sick, or haven't had time to prepare, for goodness sake, sit down and let the choir take over. At least they have rehearsed and are not ill.

2. *Fallacy of irrelevance*—where one has a good story or anecdote that we must get off our chest, but which has no bearing on the issue at hand. Thus, we have to fight our listeners' minds away from that good story or anecdote in order to win them for the issue at hand. If the bed is hard from then on, we make it so.

3. *Fallacy of ambiguity*—where one is impressed with one's success in having a good introduction, which we will use again for another sermon out of town. Such hash-making is usually the menu of the indolent or the falsely proud.

4. *Fallacy of Red Skeltonism*—where preachers confuse themselves with comedians, feeling that winning attention and interest must come only through an anecdote. The joke is really on the preacher because Red Skelton told the joke much better.

5. *Fallacy of double doism*—where the preacher specializes in porch-building rather than house-building. Usually, they build two or three front porches to all of their houses, as if

the congregation would rather linger on the porches than live in the house.

6. *Fallacy of schizophrenic intellectualism*—where preachers feel that they will speak to the "intellectuals" in the congregation first through a technical, theological dissertation on biblical hermeneutics, and then go on to pick up "Aunt Jane" in the conclusion by going over the river and through the woods. Little do they realize that the whole sermon should be for all the people. All laity (intellectuals and non-intellectuals) are babies in regard to technical jargon. All laity (intellectuals and nonintellectuals) have minds needing illumination, hearts needing warming, and souls needing to be set on fire with God's word.

THE SERMONIC PROPOSITION
Definition of It

My opening judgment about the nature of *propositions* is similar to the one about *sermonic introductions,* affirming that the *proposition* is not only important but is also *essential* to a sermon. It is the very heart of a sermon. ***IF YOU AIN'T GOT NO PROPOSITION, THEN YOU AIN'T GOT NO SERMON, NEITHER.*** Without a *proposition* there is no sermon, even if you been up there in the pulpit for years. No *proposition* is the basis for my judgment of contemporary preaching being "shallow and in the shadows."

"In the beginning is the (propositional) idea; and, the (propositional) idea *is* the sermon; and, without a (propositional) idea, no sermon is made that was made"— H. Grady Davis and I are singing a duet. And you too support this thesis. Your being here taking this whipping from me means that you have a stake in preaching, or you are crazy. Everybody here (except fools) must have some basic questions resounding in their being by now.

Proposition

Since we have said "in truth" that the *proposition* is essential to a sermon (*why* from the introduction), and since it is obvious that we-all have a deep concern about this preaching business (more *why* picked up), and since I have been staking the claim that *"If you ain't got no proposition, then you ain't got no sermon, neither"* (still some more *why* added)—if all of the above is really true, then we need to consider in depth this weightier matter of preaching law (the *what* of subject picked up) in terms of some basic questions about its necessary existence in our preaching (the *how* for the *body* being suggested). Thus, we-all can be up and about our heavenly Father's business in conveying the homily of God rightly to the deepest needs of sin-sick souls in our times for their ultimate liberation (the *what for* for the *conclusion* being suggested).

A sentence definition: The *proposition* is the central, integrating, controlling sentence of the discourse, embracing a clear, procedural *how* being added to an already established *what* and *why* of the discourse, so that the hearers can comprehend the entire meaning of the discourse through that central, integrating, controlling sentence. The uniqueness of the *proposition* is that it is the only place where the *how* for the whole sermon can be found. Also, the *proposition* is unique in that it is the wedding, the only place where *why* and *what* and *how* are combined. Note the three *why* clauses in the *proposition*—since it is "essential," since we have an "ultimate concern," and since without it we ain't got "no sermon, neither." The phrase "weightier matter of preaching law" is *what*, being a synonym of the title—the *sermonic proposition*. The *how*, found in the expression "in terms of some basic questions about its necessary existence in preaching," suggests the points for the *body*. *What for*, something new, since it has not been given anywhere else yet—"so that we-all can be up and about . . . liberation," is what the *conclusion* will be about. People need to be in the complete know on the issues, which is why we say again: ***IF YOU AIN'T GOT NO PROPOSITION, THEN YOU AIN'T GOT NO SERMON WORTH A DIME, NEITHER.***

The *proposition* relates to every other element of the sermon. Every element in essence is found in it, so that we can see the whole sermon in a nutshell in the *proposition*. The metaphysical significance is that the *proposition* has to do with making the central claim for the whole sermon, in terms of the will of God being declared in it, for the purpose of the hearers responding to that central claim.

A young buck argued with me over whether or not a *proposition* was really presented in his sermon, with the young buck proving he had one, as follows:

One sentence: "God the Father is real nice."

Another sentence: "God the Son is real nice." (Says this one is the *proposition*)

Another sentence: "God the Holy Spirit is real nice."

I refute this young buck's "Amazing Disgrace" because these sentences are three pieces of something in a sack, none of which are worth choosing. No question raised at all. No argument. No help at all to sick people. No look toward heaven. I further refute this young buck's "Amazing Disgrace" because all the sentences have the same metaphysical weight. It is bound to be missed, since none can be the *proposition,* in that the *proposition* must be unique among sentences.

Nonpropositional sentences are just like a man running his mouth and saying nothing, with nobody bothering him, since there is no claim to react to. Propositional sentences are just like Jesus running his mouth and saying something. Some heard him gladly and were saved, while others heard him madly and hanged him, since there were claims to be reacted to.

Propositional significance in sermons has to do with our always making central, metaphysical, divine claims for the whole sermon about divine reality incumbent upon us, since we are always talking about much more than the weather on that preaching stage.

There are three reasons *why* the proposition is a necessity, *why* it must be. The big question that can lead to deeper understanding of this weighty matter of the preaching law is relative to the "preacher him/herself," to the "sermon per se," and to the "listening congregation." Time will permit only one to be dealt with here—the congregational need for wholeness.

Broken people out there before us need to see something whole, so that they can be made whole. The *proposition* is the one place to see the sermon whole, the place where the congregation can understand the sermon fully. An example of need for wholeness is in the Transfiguration scene. Jesus showed his disciples the whole meaning of God in history. Jesus needed to do this, since most people felt that Jesus' different technique was undermining the faith of old. At the scene of Transfiguration, Moses, the Great Emancipator, was there, saying, "Jesus is a-okay." Elijah, the Great Prophet, was there, saying, "Jesus is a-okay." Jesus, the Great Redeemer, was there to fulfill their dreams.

In my personal experience, I understood the need for wholeness and found meaning while working cleaning toilets and urinals at the National Biscuit Company before going to Boston University. I saw the relation of that job to the health of kids licking ice cream from the ice cream cones made by the company. Also, I saw the relation of that job as a means to this end. I looked over the mountain, children, and saw the rest of the proposition for my life. I now enjoy profoundly what I am doing and would do that job all over again, gladly—since I saw and still see the rest of the *proposition* for my life.

So, ladies and gentlemen of the jury, as the defense, I rest my case on that one reason *why* we must have a *proposition* in all of our sermons. Broken people listening to us desperately need to hear something whole, so that they can be made whole in the depths of their being. I have tried to prove this beyond a reasonable doubt in this one reason presented. But, ladies and gentlemen of the jury, it is now your task to decide whether you will exonerate this propositional client to return to its rightful place at the heart of all your preaching.

Types of Propositions

1. *Numerical indication.* The stated number of points is the directive, such as "I shall discuss the kindness of God from *three* points of view."

2. *Topical indication.* The *gist* of the points is the directive, such as "I shall discuss the kindness of God in terms of creation, providence, and redemption."

3. *Purpose indication.* The *overall intention* is the directive, such as "It shall be my endeavor to show that the kindness of God shines through all of God's works in an infinite degree."

These basic principles should be learned, then one must develop them into rich and complex varieties of propositions.

The Location of the Proposition

The *proposition* can be the first sentence—*before* the introduction—or the sentence *after* the introduction, but it must come before the *body*.

Common Errors Regarding Propositions

1. *Fallacy of Sherlock Holmesism.* Where one has the false notion that a congregation is to be kept in the dark about the truth of God until the very end. Thus the preacher carries them through all the "vanity of vanities" until the end, where the preacher will declare the whole matter. God's truth is enough of a mystery without the preacher deliberately making it more mysterious.

2. *The sin of omission.* Where the preacher is broad-minded and does not lead the congregation to a definite assertion about a controversial issue. Unlike Joshua, the preacher is too much of a jellyfish to state the *proposition* upon which the preacher stands, or the one that is suggested in the text.

3. *Fallacy of parrotism.* Where an individual is victimized by the "holy three" in sermonizing. Over and over again, each and every Sunday, the preacher relies on the numerical indicator to the exclusion of the rest.

4. *Fallacy of dwarfism.* Where individuals never develop their grammatical powers, so that rich, complex kinds of propositional sentences might be stated. These fellows stick to simple sentences. Sometimes the simple is only for the "simple."

9

Definition, Elaboration, and Exemplification of the Sermonic Body

*Definition is a one-sentence statement embracing the essential comprehensive meaning of an issue in a nutshell, the overall sense of the **what, how, and why**.*

Elaboration is a follow-up concern of what more specifically the definition implies. Supporting sentences are used to spell out in detail the implications of the discourse, so that hearers can get a firmer grip on its living significance very soon in the discussion.

Exemplification is another way of being specific about how the definition relates to concrete instances, so that hearers can get the flesh-and-blood sense of the practical value of an issue as being relevant for life.

NOW, IN YOUR GENERAL INTERPRETATION, you need to be clear that two kinds of questions will abide in the development of a complete sermonic idea. One kind of question is the discursive or discussional kind of question, which calls for answering in-depth on the issue. The second is the indicative or definitional kind of question which calls for answering briefly, but comprehensively, on the issue in a sentence. In general, these two kinds of questions will abide when selecting and developing a complete sermonic idea.

DEFINITION

More specifically, the first element of a discussional answer to our sermonic question, namely, *definition*, calls for getting at a precise meaning of what the whole issue is all about, by means of that first comprehensive sentence of the discussion, so that people can be put in-the-know comprehensively, at the get-go of the sermon. The factor of comprehensiveness involves answers to basic questions about the item being defined, in terms of *what, how,* and *why* of the issue, so that a complete picture of the issue is given in a nut-shell in the definition sentence. It is absolutely necessary to have a meaningful definition at the beginning of a discussion for people to get the comprehensive sense of your message or they should bring a brick to church with them for knocking you down on your rump for trying to talk without a comprehensive sentence.

The first thing called for in a discussion is always definition. To define literally means this, when broken down into its component parts: the prefix *de-* means "down," and *fine* means "end" or "fin-ish." So, literally speaking, to define means to cover what the whole issue is about immediately; to give an overarching, umbrella-type sentence of what the overall meaning of the issue is.

Now, the rest of this stuff is merely going to be repetition. To define means to cover what the whole issue is all about immedi-ately (now that is saying the same thing again in another way); to determine the boundaries of an issue right away (so, I said it another way, didn't I?); to get a comprehensive sense of what the overall meaning is all about (said it again in another way); in that first comprehensive over-arching, umbrella-type sentence for immediate comprehending purpose. I said the same thing in the last sentence that I said in the other sentences. I just said it a dif-ferent way each time. When you are talking to the ear you have got to repeat, that is how you get elaboration done, through repetition.

Definition means to reveal the content as well as the context in which the whole discussion will be cast to begin with, repeating again, getting down to the end of the issue in-question and under-question, by means of a nutshell statement at the outset for all to comprehend. In a word, definition means having answers to the questions of *what* and *how* and *why* about the issue at that begin-ning comprehensive statement. I am merely saying the same thing in different ways. I was talking to your ears, wasn't I?

Meaning and Manner of Definition

MEANING OF DEFINITION—FOURFOLD

1. To *limit*—by setting a boundary-of-meaning around a term, so that when the term in question is referred to in the process of communicating it, all parties understand the term to mean *this*, and *only this*, and nothing else. For example, in the process of communicating about a cat, all involved should understand that the discussion refers to *this only*: a four-legged, furry, long-tailed mammal, approximately nine inches tall, eighteen inches long, and four inches wide, which eats mice, loves milk, and says "Meow." Any creature not fitting that description should not come to mind when they are discussing a cat. The ideas in their minds should be *limited* to that, and only that, and nothing else in their cat discussion.

2. To *fixate*—by agreeing to make the term *stand still* rather than rambling around to mean other things at another time or in another setting, so that whenever and wherever the term in question is used it is *always* there in the *same place* with the *same meaning* on the shelf. In other words, to define means to establish a stationary target of meaning rather than having a moving and hide-and-go-seek target, because defining means to nail something down to a fixed position, so that it can be conveniently located anytime and anywhere.

3. To *concretize*—by taking the idea out of abstraction and thin air, so that it can have the kind of flesh-and-blood, *down-to-earth meaning* that can be dealt with by the majority of sane people with whom we communicate. In the defining process an idea becomes *flesh*, that is, becomes *incarnated into earthly experience* through the virgin of definition.

   For example, if the other persons in the cat discussion were from Mars and had never seen a cat, but were made aware of the *concrete qualities* given in our exemplary statement above, then—even in the absence of seeing a cat—the other persons could have some kind of concrete idea about a cat.

For instance, is not the concretizing process what happens when a criminal is apprehended in another city by means of a description, even though the cops had not known that thug before? To define means to concretize an issue, so that the unknown can be known and dealt with in a down-to-earth, matter-of-fact way.

4. To *equate*—by expressing the meaning of the term in question in *other words*, so that the term can be identified with concepts *already known* that mean the *same* thing.

For example, to define by saying that a cat is a cat ain't clearing up nothing about what a cat is by definition, if the folk don't know what a cat is to begin with. If they already know what a cat is, that kind of definition would be adding exactly nothing but "stainky" breath to the discussion. We could make the unknown cat better understood by *equating* it with *known qualities*, as we did above: a cat is a four-legged, furry, long-tailed mammal, approximately nine inches tall, eighteen inches long, and four inches wide, which eats mice, loves milk, and says "Meow." To define means to *equate* the known item to things and qualities already known, which is why we need to be versatile in knowing other words.

MANNER OF DEFINITION—TWOFOLD

1. *Substantive manner of defining.* The issue is *explained* in terms of its *material* or *stuff* or *nature* (substance), so that it can be understood in terms of *what it is* (i.e., four-legged, furry, long-tailed mammal, approximately nine inches tall, eighteen inches long, and four inches wide = substance of a cat).

2. *Dynamic manner of defining.* The issue is explained in terms of its *method of operations* (M.O.) or *functions* or *actions* (dynamic), so that it can be understood in terms of *how it operates* (i.e., eating mice, loving milk, and saying "Meow" = functions of a cat).

Now, there are profound reasons why this issue of *definition* must be set forth at the beginning of our discussion. For instance, one reason *why*—among many reasons—some of us can't preach worth a dime, in terms of people getting a meaningful message for their living, is that we are too idiotic to recognize the significance of this definitional need at the outset of our *dis-gusting* the issues with them.

Some of us are often so idiotically preoccupied with running our mouths about *how* those folks can do and about *why* those folks should do that, without a clear definition of *what* "dis and dat" are all about at the get-go. The people out there in the pews usually don't know *what* it is by definition that we are talking about. That is the reason why so many of them are often sitting up there batting their eyes kind-a-foolish-like, while we "is" driving home that effective *how* point and that strong *why* point in our discussion of the issues.

Far more often, they are baffled and confused and completely in the dark about *what it is by definition* we are running our mouths about. They leave the church many-a-day unedified by the distinct absence of the primary definitional *what* consideration in our light-chat from the pulpit. They live their lives many-a-year having heard no clear word from the Lord, since they cannot get a grip on what we are trying to say in the name of the Lord.

And maybe, just maybe, that accounts for why so many people in the pews don't know a thing else to do except to cut a fool on them *bainches*, even after forty years of hearing our so-called *powvuhful soimons*. If the jackleg up there in the pulpit with a nasty collar on backwards ain't making no comprehensive sense, then what else are they supposed to do, except to find something to play with to entertain their bored selves.

So that is one justifiable reason for defining the issue at the get-go. If the members of the congregation don't get *what* we are talking about on that preaching stage, then our preaching is bound to be in vain, except for those who cut the fool on *them bainches* in some kind of entertaining play. At least, they can have a dance. That is at least something for paying dumb jacklegs.

Everybody knows, or should know, that another reason *why* you need a comprehensive statement at the front of your discussion is so that *'Fessor Clawk* can tell at the *git-go* whether or not we *younguns* know what we are talking about in our sermons. *"Yeah, Man, we done loined a lot from 'Fessor Clawk."*

Therefore, it looks like that by grasping the significance of the definitional sentence in setting up a sound discussion, we done found ourselves some *kine* of rich gold mine with a gushing oil well right beside it. And we *gon* let this gold mine and oil well support us the rest of the way, so that we won't have to work so hard on those other three discussional issues (*elaboration, exemplification,* and *justification*) coming up.

Professionals of the Word of God ain't got no business *killin'* ourselves *woikin' lak* a fool, especially when we have found ourselves a gold mine and an oil well rich enough to take care of ourselves and our posterity. So if any of you get stuck on the rest of this discussional journey, stuck out there on this discussional highway with your discussional car broke down and without a discussional penny in your pocket, just call either this discussional gold mine or this discussional oil well found in the Yellow Pages of this lecture for some help, calling any time night or day, or from anywhere collect.

ELABORATION

Now, watch carefully and closely, because you are going to learn something today. We come now to a second specific thing called for by a meaningful discussion of the issue, namely, *elaboration.* Elaboration is always a followup concern on what the definitional sentence, *what, how,* and *why,* implies or suggests by means of other supporting sentences. The elaboration spells out the meaning of the *definition* in detail, so that your readers or hearers can get a firmer grip on *what* that definition implies specifically, real soon, in a meaningful discussion for their living. To elaborate— watch closely—literally means this: when broken down into its component parts. The prefix *e-* means what? "From." And *laborate* means what? "Work" or "sweat." You can see the word *labor.* That means you ain't at the playground; you are at the sweatshop. So, literally speaking, elaborate means to work or sweat or slave over something in order to produce a greater meaning of it. But in this case, in this discussional case, it means more specifically that you work and sweat and slave, if you will, to produce a fuller understanding of what that definitional sentence suggests by implication.

To elaborate means that you explain your definition with other supporting sentences in elaborational paragraphs for the congregation's living knowledge in the daily drama of life. It means to sweat in taking the goodie out of that definitional nutshell, so that we, and others, can get at that definitional goodie for our daily living. We cannot eat that definitional goodie in that definitional nutshell. We never do eat nuts in a nutshell, do we? We must take it out of that nutshell. Elaboration, then, is getting that definitional goodie out of that definitional nutshell for eating and living purposes. It is working it out of that definitional nutshell in sweaty, slavish activities with supporting sentences, as a nutpicker for eating that definitional goodie for meaningful strength in our living existences. Does this make any sense to you?

In a word, whereas definition makes it possible to comprehend with the mind *what* that issue is all about in general for mental understanding, elaboration makes it possible to comprehend with the mind *what that issue implies in detail*, specifically, for mental knowledge, for actually living the meaning of that defined understanding in the drama of life. Definition is the overall part for understanding. Elaboration is the specific part for living. Definition opens up the *what* so that the mind can embrace the meaning of it in a comprehensive way. Elaboration is the specific part, so that we can see *how* this thing works it out in the day-to-day drama of life. Does that make any sense to you? Thank you, Jesus, and thank y'all for your help.

Now, as an example of elaboration, let us refer to two distinctive kinds of elaboration for two kinds of communication.

For instance, we need to be aware that there are two basic ways of elaborating relative to basic types of communicating objectives. You have got two objectives and there are two ways to get to those objectives, so that we can get the maximum communicative efficiency out of knowing about both ways of elaborating those two objectives.

Now, one basic way of elaborating has to do with communication to the ear, orally, in a manner in which the ear picks up meaning best. With the hope of utilizing this type of communication, let us return to my elaboration on the definitional aspects of discussion, so as to get some idea, at least from my poor effort, on how to elaborate for the ear with maximum effect. Alright, definitional part.

The major factor in elaborating for the ear is repetition of the definition in different ways, since the ear is dependent on the speaker to keep it reminded from time to time of *what* the definition is about in oral elaboration. When you are up there in the pulpit, and the people don't have a manuscript, it means that they are dependent on you to keep in their minds what the issue is about. So, you have got to repeat. In the listening situation the hearer does not have a copy of the definition to refer to in order to remind himself or herself of what the definition is about. The speaker must do the reminding through repetition, if the listeners are going to get the meaning of the definition into their system through their ears.

Another basic way of elaborating has to do with communicating to the eye, by writing in a manner in which the eye picks up meaning best. In this type of communication, let us endeavor to elaborate a bit on my definition of *contract*, so as to get some idea, at least of my poor definition, on how to elaborate for the eye with maximum effect. I will give you a definition of contract. Then, I am going to elaborate this definition for the eye.

A contract is a foundational agreement or guideline, understood by all concerned in a binding way for working together with some reasonable degree of harmony and creativity. In the reading situation, the problem is not whether the definition has been heard, because you ain't hearing it, you are looking at it with your eyes. It is what we were talking about before. When you are looking at it with your eyes, it doesn't matter whether or not you heard it. It is seeing it, isn't it? The issue is not whether it has been heard, as in the hearing situation, but whether it has been understood, since the reader can read and reread the definition to be reminded of it. So, the major issue in the reading situation is not repetition but explanation of the definition.

The major issue in the reading situation would be to raise a question as to whether the *what*, or the *how*, or the *why* parts of the written definition would be the most problematic for the reader's correct understanding. So when you write a definition for someone to read, you stand back off of it and ask yourself, "Now, which part of this definition might the reader not understand?" That is the part you are going to elaborate. You may not have to elaborate all three elements, because if all three parts are confusing then you need another definition. But you stand back and ask, Which is the most problematic thing here that might be misunderstood? Then you go ahead and elaborate that part. You ain't got to repeat it because your audience can read it. But ask yourself, What might they misunderstand in this definition? Would it be the *what* part or the *how* part or the *why* part?

Now, in my definition of *contract* I believe that the problematic thing would be the *what* part, the foundational agreement or guideline. I believe that my readers would want to know—What do I mean by foundational agreement or guideline? I think that you can understand what I mean in the *how*—about mutually understood in a binding way. I think that you can understand the *why*—for working together for some reasonable degree of creativity and harmony. The readers can understand the *how* and *why*, but they might not understand *what* I mean when I use the words *foundational agreement* or *guideline*. So that is the part that I am going to elaborate for the eye of my readers.

Listen, when you write a sermon for me, because you are writing for my eyes, I want you to look at your definition and when you see what might be problematic, then that is what you elaborate. Start off by saying, "Now, what I mean by such and such a thing is . . ." It could be the *how* part or the *why* part, or it could be the *what* part. You have got to stand back and make a judgment at what is going to be the rough thing for Doc to comprehend because I don't want Doc to misunderstand me, so I'm going to elaborate. In this definition of *contract* it happens to be the *what* part, I think. Does that make any sense to you?

Now, I told you *what* elaboration is, and I have told you *how* it is, haven't I? There are two kinds of elaboration, one for the ear of the listener, the other for the eye of the reader. Now I am going to tell you *why* we need to be elaborating on the issue all the time. Ain't that the way we are suppose to discuss?

Let me say at the outset that I will be very brief in this rationale for stating the necessity for elaborating the issue. There are two reasons for demanding the slavish, elaboration activity in our discussions of the issue all the time. One reason is the need for depth in your educational process by means of practice in thinking through issues deeply, so that the well-being of both the student and your future hearers can benefit in depth from your relevant education in depth. Is this not the main reason that you came to this school in the first place? Being here primarily to drink deeply of knowledge so that you can be more effective in serving black folks more relevantly? Is that not the main reason why you came to ITC in the first place? To drink deeply of knowledge at this fountain of learning in order to help others more efficiently and relevantly in your ministry?

Thus, because of your need to drink deeply of knowledge for helping others efficiently and relevantly, I demand that you be up and about this holy business of slaving out in detail the elaboration of the issues in your holy sermons. I don't give you an exam for passing and flunking. I give exams so that you get some practice for your preaching. You will have to do in your preaching the same thing that I will have you do in your sermon preparation assignments. You have got to define your points, not hope that the congregation gets them. YOU HAVE GOT TO DEFINE YOUR BODY POINTS! Spell them out for the ear. Repeat it, and repeat it again until they get the thesis of that point. Yes, siree! That is why I have you do that. It ain't for no play. You got to do it with every idea, so that they get the overall understanding of *what* it specifically means for living, and *how* you are going to live this in life, and *why* you need to buy it. If you don't do it that way in preaching, then you can't sell nothing! This ain't no play period. This is for your ministry.

Now, a second reason why I demand this slavish elaborational activity in your discussion of the issue is the need for personal growth in your educational process by means of practice in expressing ideas in your own authentic way, so that you can live among people and be accepted as the authentic person in the name of the Lord. Is that not the main trouble with the average young monkey in school, and especially in a theological graduate school, especially in Dr. Clark's class, always repeating my expressions all the time? Get some of your own expressions and let mine go unless you are going to pay me some money for repeating what I say. That's right.

Do we not find that all too many young theological monkeys merely quote and 'peat' from somebody else's definition like a polly parrot? Just because I get sick and tired of young polly parrots with your continuous quote and 'peat' mess, I demand that you begin to grow up in your thinking and speaking on the issue as whole, mature persons speaking in your own way authentically. You ain't got no business trying to lead nobody nowhere if you are not able to think and to speak in relevant creative ways to the new surprising situations confronting leaders and their followers daily across a dangerous wilderness toward the city of our God.

I have got to prepare you for every eventuality. You got to be able in any situation to think authentically about the different situations that you confront in life. These two reasons survive as the necessity of elaborating the issue—educational depth and maturational development are the definitive reasons for being competent and relevant in these times for black folks and others.

EXEMPLIFICATION

A third thing called for in a discussion of questions is *exemplification*, which is another way of expressing something deep about how that definition applies, by means of relating that heavenly idea in the definition to a concrete, particular, down-to-earth situation (that is *how* you do it) so that your audience can really get a firm grip on how that heavenly meaning can apply to him or her in a more practical way for their living.

For instance, even from the term itself, we get a suggestion about a more practical way of making a heavenly idea clear for living on earth. To exemplify literally means this when broken down into its component parts: the prefix *ex-* means what? "From," "out," or "from out of." Emplify/amplify means what? "Clear or lighted." Literally speaking, it means to make something clear or to put a light on something that is in the dark in order to see how it works in a specific instance so that we can know how to use it in the practical affairs of our living.

Isn't that what I did a minute ago with that definition elaboration, telling you how to do that thing when you are doing it for the ear, and how to do this principle when you are doing it for the eye? In a word, it means to show how our ideas apply to life by making our ideas become concrete for ourselves and others, so that we are able to practice those ideas in the daily drama of our living.

Both you and I should really see that the issue is relevant for practical living, by means of a well-illuminated, well-clarified exemplification of the issue in question and under question in the name of the Lord. Now as we illustrate what we mean by the third element in our discussion called definition, I want you to use this presentation on definition as if it is the Yellow Pages, so that you can get some professional help when you need it on discussing an idea. So that is the *how* of it. You know *what* it is. You know *how* it is. So, what is the next question? *Why* is it? Let's go on to the *why* of it.

Why, then, is the exemplification of the issues necessary in a creative discussion? *Why* must we be able to exemplify the issues? Well, there are two reasons for demanding this clarifying, illuminating, exemplificating activity in your discussion of the issues in your preaching. Watch me carefully, now.

One reason for this necessary activity of exemplifying has to do with people on earth needing to see heavenly ideas down on the ground in order for them to be able to use them in a practical, beneficial way in their daily living. Most people, most *menses* and *womenses*, cannot simply dig or grab an abstract idea in the air with their peanut heads. You know that. Most people cannot grab mathematics, logic, and philosophy, and things like that because they are abstracts in the air and their minds can't get it. Most *menses* and *womenses* cannot deal with no spiritual idea floating around in the air. And that is what we are talking about. When you preach you are talking about spiritual ideas. And you can't grab on to spiritual ideas floating around in the air by trying to catch it out of the air with your peanut head alone as a catcher's mitt. You will be making errors in life all the time if you have to catch God's word out of the air with your peanut head alone as the glove for catching it.

For instance, I recall coaching the students' wives' softball team while a student in seminary, and why they asked me, I do not know. Maybe, they thought that I sound like a coach because of my voice. I'll admit that either I sound like a coach or they thought that I knew all about the game because of my talking about it so much. Maybe, that is why they chose me. Or maybe because I could play fairly well. I could take care of my position. I do not know for sure why they asked me to be their coach but they did.

I recall one wife who could not catch anything in the air. She could run and pick up a grounder after it stopped rolling a mile away, but she could not deal with a fly ball in the air no kind of way. She would miss a fly ball every time. So I put her in right field and prayed to God that the other team had no left-handed batters so that no fly balls would ever be hit in right field.

Now, we had some other wives worse than she was, who couldn't catch nothing in the air either, and would merely walk after the ball after it stopped rolling a mile a way. They couldn't catch a fly ball and then they would walk after it. So she was better than some other wives that we had trying to make the team. So she made the team because of her hustle in running after the ball that had stopped a mile away which she had missed catching. At least she was faithful and had some team spirit expressed in running after a missed fly ball with enthusiasm. But the other wives wouldn't even do that. They would miss it and walk after it, but she would run after it. Because of her team spirit, I let her make my ball team.

Anyway, there are two outs and the last inning with the score 4 to 1 in our favor, with the bases loaded for the other team and a fly ball was hit to right field. Just put down four runs for them. Just start getting the bats and balls together and head your buncom-buncom home in defeat. Because the game was automatically over when that fly ball headed for right field. The announcer would be saying, "NOW, A HIGH FLY BALL IS GOING OUT INTO RIGHT FIELD." And the coach would be saying "SHIT!" because she wasn't going to catch it in the air. The ball has got to hit the ground and then she got to run after it and get it when it stopped rolling a mile away. And while she was chasing after that fly ball a mile away, all those other women on that other team are going to be hooking around those bases. It would be four runs for them if an ordinary fly ball was hit to right field. So just get set to head your buncom-buncom home in defeat. Don't waste your breath praying to God for an accident, that a miracle might happen. Just get the damn equipment together. Get all our stuff together and carry your buncom-buncom home in defeat, because she ain't never caught no fly ball in the air, no kind of way in her faithful life.

Well now, well now, most *menses* and *womenses* are just like that woman on my team when it comes to grasping God's word out of the air with their peanut heads alone as the catcher's mitt. They will miss God's word every time if it is left in the air by us in the abstract. So it has got to be some kind of easy grounder for most *menses* and *womenses* to catch it. It has got to be down on the ground for most *menses* and *womenses* to be able to see that it is a relevant gospel ball game for their practical living in the drama of life. Another way of putting it is that it has got to be down on the ground just like old mangy Rover the dog's eating bowl. So that old mangy Rover the dog can really wag his tail as he gets at that practical benefit of that nourishing food down on the ground in his feeding bowl. Most people are just like that dog, they cannot climb to heavenly heights until that gospel food is down on the ground in some kind of eating bowl for their practical living.

And hear me, when I say that even our God, even our God, finally had to recognize that most of us would never get the heavenly message in the air rightly, unless God made it walk and talk in human flesh, down on the ground, in a practical, concrete example in Jesus Christ. God kept throwing us fly balls in the air but most of us missed them every time. Thus, our God finally rolled us an easy grounder in Jesus Christ. Our God put it down on the ground in Jesus Christ and made it easy enough for everybody to catch the ball that God threw to us in Jesus Christ, if they really wanted to play ball with our Lord. And because our God finally put that stuff down on the ground in an easy grounder in Jesus Christ, even bad players like you and me have been able to make God's ball team. Hallelujah! When God put that spiritual food down on

the ground in our spiritual eating bowls so that even dumb suckers could get at it and our tails have been wag, wag, wag like
Rover's ever since.

Hallelujah! Praise God! When it is down on the ground we can
get it. That is why I have been giving you these lectures each day.
I have been trying to roll you some easy grounders with these lectures and examples so that you can see what I am talking about as
well as hear it, so that all of you can make the team in this class.
We still got some dumb players in here so I throw you some easy
grounders so that you too can make the team. I have been putting
this homiletical food down on the ground for you with these lectures so that your tail can go wag, wag, wag just like Rover's in this
class. Come and dine, the master is calling to you in here while
this homiletical food is being served down on the ground.

10

Sermonic Clarification

Sermonic clarification is concerned with using earthly, pic-
turesque language to delineate in dramatic fashion an analogy,
so that by using every part of the story hearers can understand
the message through their feelings as well as through their
thinking.

TODAY, WE COME TO *CLARIFICATION*, the illuminative consideration of the idea, which is the development of as much common understanding about the idea as possible. That statement points to a basic function that the sermonic body must necessarily perform for the sermonic proposition. If the sermonic body is earning its right to breathe, and eat, and dwell in the affairs of humans, it must develop as much clarifying light about the propositional idea as possible for clarified living, since its very existence is for being *the more light functionaire* for the sermonic idea.

Now, what do we mean by the sermonic body being *the more light functionaire* for the sermonic idea? We can get a clearer meaning of this *more light* implication by looking at the literal meaning of the term clarification. The term *clarification* literally means "to make clear," "to make pure," "to make transparent," "to throw light upon something unclear," in the dark. Again, for instance, the term *clarification* is closely associated with such terms as *illustrate* and *illuminate;* the roots of those terms, *lus* and *lum,* always mean to make something *shine, glow, light up.* The term *clarification* is also associated with such terms as *example* and *amplify* with the root *amp*— like how many amps you got? To clarify means always lighting up something, to make it clear and pure and shining. If you ain't got no amps, ain't no use of you trying to drive no car.

126

So "clarificationly" speaking, the sermonic body is similar to what floodlights are at a night football game with those floodlights making it possible for the players to perform on a football field with meaning rather than running around in the dark wondering who got the ball or where the goal line is. So you can't play no meaningful night football game in life nor any other meaningful game in life under darkened, unclarified conditions. Illumination in your mind enables you to know truth in order to commit yourself to it. And this is what we are talking about here. You can't play no meaningful game in life without first having some illumination in your mind.

Nobody tries to play a night football game in the dark without clarifying floodlights. Nobody tried to do that unless you are talking about what often happens at some *cullud* schools, where you might play any kind of way, with or without floodlights at a night football game.

For example, I remember how it was at that *cullud* school where I was dean out there in Texas. We tried to play football games under all kinds of unclarifying conditions at that *cullud* school with our players only getting black-eyed peas and fatback to eat, while those other players from those state schools were getting steak and caviar. Our players were out there ragged and ill-equipped, while those other players from those state schools had everything.

We at that *cullud* school tried to play football under all kinds of unclarifying conditions. Our players were out there on that field, scared to death to bend over because everybody in the grandstands could see all the way up to their tonsils. Our players were out there on that field scared to tackle less those ragged shoulder pads rip from shore to shore like saw dust. Our players were out there on that field naked, scared, and hungry, trying to hold up the honor of their school under unclarifying conditions.

And not only that, the players were out there naked and hungry and scared but all of us in the grandstands at that *cullud* school were also scared to death of being embarrassed at our night football games. All of us in the grandstands were nervous and scared too, in addition to our boys, since we were never sure when the electric company would come to turn off the electricity for never having paid our electric bill on time. The business manager acted like he never had an electric bill in his office, so he never paid it on time.

So under those kinds of unclarifying conditions, it is not surprising at all that our team never did win a football game, with them being out there on that field—hungry and naked and all of us nervous about when those lights might go off to our school's embarrassment at our night football game. You can't play any meaningful football games under unclarified conditions like that. Those young boys of ours had no business out there trying to hold up the honor of their *alma mater* under those unclarifying conditions in the first place.

So I made at least one creative contribution while at that *cullud* school out there in Texas. I used my influence and position to put a stop to that slaughter of our hungry, half-naked, and nervous boys by seeing to it that we quit playing football until we could afford it, because ain't nobody got no business trying to hold up the honor of the *alma mater* under no hellish unclarifying conditions like that. It was not fair to our young boys to try to play like that, with nothing to work with.

By the same token, we are saying here that you cannot play a meaningful sermonic game in life under hellish, unclarified darkened conditions like that, neither. Your congregation needs a set of clarifying floodlights on that propositional game. They need a set of clarifying floodlights with a paid up light bill so that their sermonic players can see clearly and know how to play that propositional game clearly in the daily drama of their living. So that is what we are trying to drive home here regarding the meaning of a clarification function of the sermonic body.

Since your hearers desperately need illustrative, exemplary materials in the body of the sermon to make the proposition clear, they need something to illuminate it, something to put floodlights on it, something to light up the life of every man, woman, and child who hears that sermon. That is exactly what the sermonic body must do for the sermonic proposition. It must clarify it. It must floodlight it, as the *more light functionaire* for the sermonic idea.

Well now, if that is what the sermonic body must be doing for the sermonic proposition, floodlighting, as the *more light functionaire*, if that floodlighting function is a basic mode of operation, the basic MO of the sermonic body, then this question begins to emerge in your minds—*how*? *How*? *How* can you carry out this illuminating, floodlighting, clarifying function in the body of the sermon? *How* can this thing be, as Nicodemus would put it? *How*? Isn't that the question? Am I dialoguing with you now? You know that you must make the sermon live, so now you want to know *how* to do it.

In response to this legitimate question of ways and means on the clarifying function of the sermonic body, I want to drive home the significance of illustration or exemplification at each point in the body of the sermon. This is how you get it done. And I want to indicate two types of illustrating or exemplifying that can be employed with clarifying indictment at each point in the body of the sermon. Did I say in the first point in the body and not in the second? IN EACH POINT IN THE BODY OF THE SERMON YOU WILL HAVE ILLUSTRATIONS OR EXEMPLIFICATION.

Now, one way of illustrating or exemplifying at each point is what I call dramatized exemplification. That is when you spell out an analogy of the point at length, and also when you make every part of the dramatized example act like a light bulb in that floodlight to participate in throwing light all over the point. Do you want to hear that again? You spell out an analogy on the point at length and you use every bit of that dramatized example to act like a light bulb in that floodlight to participate in throwing light all over the point. Yes, you have a big floodlight, but you have to make sure that each bulb in that floodlight is doing its part.

I am trying to impress upon you the necessity of having a comprehensive proposition in all of your sermonizing as we wrestle with the *why* of the sermonic proposition. You ask the question, *WHY HAVE YOU GOT TO HAVE ONE?* And, I am giving you the answer in a dramatized example.

For instance, you need to get from Washington, D.C., to New York City by bus. And the considerate station announcer gives you the proposition about two buses in lane number 3 and lane number 4, both headed for New York, but with different intermittent stops, so that you will be able to get on the right bus to get to your destination on time, to attend your tenth cousin's funeral, since he jumped up and died on you like a dirty dog between pay days.

Not only do you dramatize that incident at length, but you also use every bit of that dramatized example to floodlight the very necessary significance of your hearers getting the rest of the proposition in your sermon, so that your hearers will also be able to get on the right sermonic bus and attend to the issues of God in the daily drama of their living.

For instance, I use that New York designation on the front of two buses as being similar to the *subject* of the sermon. I use the different routes that the two buses will travel as being similar to the different ways the same subject can be asserted by differing sermonic propositions. I use your confusion about the two New York buses as being similar to your hearers' confusion when they don't know the rest of the proposition in your preaching. I use your joy in hearing that station announcer giving the rest of the proposition about that bus in lane number 3 as being similar to your hearers' joy at getting a full comprehensive proposition about our sermonic buses from us. And I use the awareness of those pagan, Gentile bus companies, of their positive need to provide this service as a judgment upon so-called holy proclaimers who are often ignorant of or unconcerned about your congregation's sermonic need in this regard. I am using every bit, all of that dramatized bus example in order to floodlight what a comprehensive, mountaintop transfigurating proposition must be in all of your sermonizing.

That dramatized bus analogy makes clear, illuminates, floodlights part by part, that which I may not have made too clear in a prosaic matter. I could have just lectured and lectured and lectured, but I used that example and saved a whole lot of talk, didn't I?

Now, why did that dramatized bus example floodlight that whole issue of propositional necessity? Was it not because I used a commonly known experience in traveling by bus, which you could see clearly as a floodlight upon the unknown propositional necessity for you, which you could not see clearly in the darkness of propositional ignorance? You knew about buses but you didn't know about propositions. You knew something about buses, so I used something that you did know about to help you understanding about propositions which you did not know about. We must use an example of something known to light up and clarify the propositional unknown. And because of that, because of the known clarifying the unknown, I am sure that at least nine out of ten of you have a deeper appreciation for the sermonic proposition in the drama of your sermonic preaching now.

Most of you now are definitely concerned about and talking about getting your proposition straight for your sermonic living. That is clear now. "Doc, I'm getting my proposition straight!" "Doc, look at my proposition and see if the proposition is all right." That dramatized example helped out a whole lot in getting across the significance of a proposition to you. Thus, I recommend dramatized exemplifications for you to be using in your preaching so that you can get sermonic body points across to your people.

Now, another way of illustrating or justifying each point in the body of the sermon is what I call undramatized, more indicative exemplification. That is where we put spotlights on many other areas by alluding to other instances to which the point also applies, in addition to the dramatized point, and where we use figures of speech, constantly, to spotlight the sermon throughout. I am not going to talk about figures of speech because you can read and study that on your own. But what I will say is that you always hear me talking in figures of speech, don't you? You hear me talking about your buncom-buncom. I am not talking about this stuff simply to tap your mind, but to hit your emotions, something you can feel. Huh? Huh? That is what we mean by figures of speech. Roar like a lion so that you feel the affects of the roar. You think I am up here to just make a fool out of myself. No, I am teaching so that you can learn something. Just like the disciples learned from Jesus, talking about such and such.

So, I am talking now about indicative or undramatized illustration or exemplification where you point to other areas where that point also applies. When you are concerned with spotlighting many other areas to which the point also applies, you merely indicate in a brief way a variety of other situations to which our floodlighting example also applies with equal power. Thus, spotlighting the other areas to which the point also applies depends on a well-put dramatized floodlighting example. You can't spotlight without a floodlight. So your floodlight has got to be working good before you can spotlight because it is the thing that makes the spotlighting significant.

Let me illustrate the significance of spotlighting other areas upon a well-put dramatized example by referring once again to our dramatized bus trip example. Now after having shown why the sermonic proposition is necessary in a meaningful preaching situation, by means of that dramatized bus example, I could have used that same floodlighting example immediately to shed its significance in areas other than meaningful preaching like this.

I talked about how it applied to preaching, but I could have talked about some connections to other places. Now this need to hear the rest of the proposition—I could have said something like this—this need to hear the rest of the proposition does not only apply to bus drivers and to listening congregations in preaching. It doesn't just apply there, because it also applies with equal force to every other meaningful situation in life, for meaningful dialogue must take place for creative living.

For seeing the rest of the proposition is desperately needed for a meaningful marriage, for understanding is crucial, unless somebody gets badly bruised in that intimate relationship. It is needed in meaningful childrearing, when the reality of a generation gap is bound to rear its ugly head when we don't dig each other's basic outlooks on life. Seeing the proposition is needed in meaningful teaching, where there must be clear understanding of all that is expected from both the teacher and the student in the teaching/learning situation. In meaningful pastoring, it is also needed. In meaningful business, it is needed. In every other meaningful situation, we must communicate comprehensively to each other for creative living together. For wherever people do not have a comprehensive understanding of each other, there, right there, is the breeding ground for animosity, violence, and human bloodshed.

I could have applied that example, on the basis of that floodlight, to every other area where creative meaning is needed, where an understanding of the proposition is needed. So, from that floodlighting example, I could have merely indicated or alluded to many other areas in a brief way to which that floodlight also applies in a powerful way.

The floodlight of meaning will make it possible to put some clarifying spotlights on a variety of other related situations as well, if it is a well-put dramatized exemplification. Thus, you need to do some indicative, spotlighting kinds of exemplifying at every point in the body of the sermon. For your hearers also need to have a clear indication of *how* that proposition applies in every area of their living.

Even more than that, your hearers need to be made aware that our divine proposition has a definite reverence to each and every soul hearing it. They definitely need to see clearly that this point applies to them as individuals, and to their own personal sin in a powerful way. Nobody got no business sitting up there when you are preaching thinking that you are not talking to them, because you turn that spotlight on everybody by indicative implication. Yes siree!

If you make the dramatized example on the young folks, then you make the indicative example on the old folks, so that the old folk don't be sitting up there grinning, thinking that you are just talking about the young. You are talking about everybody in the church house. So, not only must you have dramatized exemplification but you must also have undramatized or indicative exemplification in a brief way, so that that floodlight shines, in a sense, on everybody there. When you are dramatizing problems in marriage, then you need to say also that this doesn't only apply to those who are married, but it also applies to single people, so that nobody is sitting up there grinning, acting like you are talking about their neighbor and that you ain't talking about them. The sermon is for everybody.

Now, that kind of floodlighting and spotlighting exemplification, making the people aware that the sermon is for them, is what it means to vocalize the claims of truth. You ain't got no business trying to preach, if the hearers never get the idea that what you are preaching about applies to them personally and individually. That is also why one of the questions you must answer in each sermon preparation has to do with suggesting ways and means to vocalize claims of truth. You ain't got no business up there trying to preach, neither, if the hearers never get the idea of *how* they can use what you are preaching about in concrete, down-to-earth, effective ways in their living. They ought to be able to see *how* they can use each point in the body of the sermon. They need to be shown in an exemplary way at each point *how* each point can be used in the daily drama of their living. They need to have a demonstration that any good salesperson would give. They need to have a demonstration at each point on *how* each point will work in a practical matter-of-fact way, which means that you must give them the kind of exemplification at each point that suggests ways and means of implementing each point in some particular way in their living. It is not just vocalizing the claims of truth that makes them aware that what you are talking about applies to them, but showing them *how* they can use each body point, if they want to try it out.

Now, bear in mind that I merely said that you must give them the kind of exemplification at each point that suggests ways and means of intimating each point with some particular way in their living. I did not say give a suggestion on every way in their living, but in some particular small way in their living. You cannot give them clues of how to do each point in every conceivable way. You do not have the time nor the ability to show them how to do everything. But you can, and must, give them at least one clue on how to get started on using each point at some particular place or time in their practical everyday living. Do not give clues on everything, but at least a clue on some small, relevant, particular area of their living at each point, to help them start implementing that point in their living.

Whether you realize it or not, that dialogical question about ways and means to do it is there in the minds of your hearers at each point. "How can I begin to do this point, Reverend?" is a living question in their minds at each point. You are not talking about doing the *how* just because Doc said it, but because you are responding to a living question in the minds of the congregation.

You tell them *what* to do, and they will get that, if you define and elaborate it clearly. And if they are sold on what you are talking about, then what is it that they will want to know? *How* can I do it? And then tell them *why*. You have got to tell them all three.

But, if you tell them to do something hard, like you ought to get on the cross, then you don't go about telling them *how* to do it, because they are not asking that question. They are going to want to know *why*. They did not go to the second question of asking *how* to do it, but *why*. What I am saying is that the *how* question is always there in their minds and you are not answering it simply because Doc said answer *what*, *how*, and *why*. You are answering it because you know that that question is out there in their minds as you talk. And a living, relevant, resurrected sermonic body always gives a small, exemplary, clarifying clue on how to begin to use that point in some particular way of their living so that the Word can begin to become flesh in the daily drama of their living under our God.

Now, let me go on, so that you know what I am talking about. We are talking about exemplification. Let me give a bad example that has nothing at all to do with vocalizing the claims of truth, of suggested ways and means, that we have been trying to set forth here. I feel an urgent need to cite this bad kind of example because some of you are so accustomed to following jacklegs that I am sure that some of you have picked up some canned mess for exemplification from unexemplary jacklegs.

I know that at the get-go some of you will not detect the fallacy in this bad example. I know that some of you will think that it is good, because some of you are so accustomed to following jacklegs, that some of you don't recognize yet, that you need a sermonic proposition in all of your preaching. I know that if you don't recognize that, then you will not recognize this.

For example, I am sure that you have all heard this kind of bad exemplifying done by a jackleg trying to shed some light on his last so-called point. And let's suppose that his last so-called point on which he is trying to shed some light for the people is this: "The significance of Jesus and the power of salvation." I said, "The significance of Jesus and the power of salvation." And I know that you have all heard something like that, and you too will try to exemplify it by following after those jacklegs. Now the jackleg is going to say something like this, as he prepares to bring that sermon home on "The Significance of Jesus and the Power of Salvation." He is about to pull the cord now with this powerful concluding example.

Um God. And great God Almighty, church let me tell you something. We need to be like that six-year-old boy going down the road one day. Six-year-old boy going down the road one day, who met a sinner man and asked him where he was going. And the sinner man said, "Son, oh, son, son where is you going?" And the little boy said, "Brother mister, brother mister, I is going fishing." And the sinner man said, "Son, son, son, you must be mistaken. How, son, is you going fishing and you ain't got no fishing pole and no worms?" The little six-year-old boy said, "Sinner man, sinner man, sinner man, I can see that you ain't been born again. Because I, I, I ain't going fishing for no fish. I am fishing for menses."

And the six-year-old boy began to tell that sinner man about the significance of Jesus. The little boy began to say, "Sinner man, sinner man, ain't nobody ever told you what Jesus said. Jesus said to follow him and that he will make us fishers of menses. So you see, sinner man, that I am going down this road following Jesus, because Jesus said that if I, if I be lifted up from the earth that I will draw all menses unto me."

Church, let me tell you this, that when that sinner man heard that child testifying to the significance of Jesus and the power of salvation, that sinner man fell down on his face and was born again that instant. And if God be God, then a little child shall lead them. Yes he did.

So Reverend Jackleg takes off from that bad example and really pulls the cord in bringing that *mess-age* home.

That is what I mean, church, just follow Jesus, just follow Jesus. Now sinners might think you are crazy going down the road without a fishing pole and no worms, but just keep on following Jesus anyhow. So that is what we got to do, church. Just like that little boy said. Lift him up, church. Lift him up, church. Lift Jesus up, church, because he said that if I be lifted up from the earth I'll draw, I'll draw, I'll draw all menses unto me.

Now, some idiots, especially some *cullud* idiots, because white idiots do other kinds of foolish things, but we are talking about the *cullud* ones now, are probably wondering why I would call that kind of example, a bad example, since so many *cullud* jacklegs have become so powerfully popular preachers and have gotten some of the best *cullud* churches by that kind of exemplifying in their preaching. So what is wrong with it, Doc? Some *cullud* idiots will think about those cavorting *cullud* crowds in *cullud* churches and will not think about the claims and demands of the Christian gospel.

Well for one thing, that kind of exemplary attempt is wrong because it is unrealistic in its choice of a preacher. A six-year-old kid should have been out shooting marbles somewhere as his calling at that age, rather than trying to preach. That kid should have had a real fishing pole and some live bait going fishing for fish rather than trying to fish for *menses*.

It is a low-down, dirty trick, it is a low-down, dirty trick on kids when ignorant grown folks try to push kids up into that pulpit just because they hear kids imitating preachers. For instance, I have heard my kids imitating me and my wife a lot of time fussing at them in their room. And they think that we don't hear them imitating the way we fuss at them. Many times I have heard that. Now, should I put my kids out on their own as adults just because I hear them imitating grown folks?

And yet, in the name of God, a lot of ignorant church folk will say nothing of robbing kids of their childhood in religion, by trying to drive kids into the pulpit just because they hear kids imitating jackleg preachers. And kids by nature will imitate anybody, including jackleg preachers. That is what a kid is, he is an imitator, trying to learn how to be an adult. The kid is just imitating and we try to shove him up in the pulpit. And then you wonder why. (This is a little psychology now to help you understand yourself.)

And, then you wonder why boy-preachers begin to act like kids when they are forty years old, after you have driven them into the pulpit for merely imitating jackleg preachers as kids. And they act like kids at forty because they have missed all the fun of being irresponsible and carefree as a kid after driving their butts up into that pulpit. And they have got to be kids at some time in their lives. Either when they are kids or when they are forty years old. They are going to be a kid sometime in their life.

Think of it, gray-headed grown folks putting the cross of redemption on kids' backs. Think of it. That gray-headed nincompoop sitting up there in the Lord's church trying to get salvation by listening to some babies in the pulpit. Jesus needs to come again. Our Lord needs to come again, not to take us back to heaven, but come again with a buggy whip to beat on some gray-headed silly butts for desecrating the house of prayer in this age by putting kids up into that pulpit. It is a low-down, dirty trick to be suggesting kid preachers. And that is one serious defect in that bad example—the preacher.

And for another thing, that kind of exemplifying attempt is wrong because it represents nothing more than the essence of a funk-show in religion. That all it is, with no implication for living the Christian life! Because if that so-called converted man on the ground, the man that fell down and was converted, if that man had asked that kid what to do next, "I'm down here and what am I going to do next, child?" If he had asked that child what to do next, that imitating kid could not have told that man on the ground a dadblasted thing to do about living the Christian life. That man would have been as dumb after he got his butt up off the ground as he was before his rump hit the deck regarding living the Christian life from then on, if he was down on the ground waiting for that kid to tell him what to do next in Jesus' name. That immature kid would not have had a dadblasted thing to say except, "Keep on following Jesus!" And lift him up anyhow in your life, imitatively. BUT FOLLOW JESUS, HOW? And lift him up, where? When it comes to those kinds of questions of meaning, that kid would have been at a loss trying to say something significant to that man on the ground. So the issue of implicative meaning for living indicates that there is something else wrong with that bad example, about a kid and a man, with the kid supposedly telling the man how to live the Christian life.

And still that kind of exemplary attempt is wrong, and this is the last one, because it is the kind of fallacy that could mislead the hearers about their witnessing function because some religious educational dropouts, of which there are many in the cullud church, some cullud religious educational dropouts, will be foolishly thinking that the way for them to witness for God is to try walking down that road without a fishing pole and no worms, literally speaking. They will not know any other way to witness, so they will be jumping to do it. And those nitwits will be sorely disappointed when sinners don't ask them where they *is* going. So that they can say, fishing for *menses* and see the power of the Lord in sinner *menses* faces when they are born again.

So, that fallacy about the genuine way to be witnessing for God . is still another thing that is wrong with that bad example. Clarifying exemplification has to do with en-lightification and not dark-ification on the issue. Light-ification for clarified living is the issue here, rather than dark-ification for running around in the blind alleys of life listening to foolish preachers. Some of you follow jacklegs too closely in this exemplary function, and that is exactly why I refer to them as darkies. That name DARKIE ain't got a thing to do with the color of a person's butt. That is not the reason I call jacklegs darkies. But it has to do with the darkie's cloudy, unclarifying mind in trying to exemplify the issue. You ain't making nothing clear—just making things dark. And that is why when you come up with examples and you make things dark in your preaching I will call you darkie that day. It ain't going to be because I am trying to be white and I am thinking of you as *cullud*, but because there is nothing but darkness coming from your words. In the meantime, I would advise you to do some further independent study on this topic so that nobody, nobody will be tempted to call you darkie in reference to your attempt to exemplify the issues in your sermonizing here or anywhere else.

You need to be clarifying the issues, in terms of vocalizing the claims of truth in specific areas of people's experiences, in terms of suggesting ways and means to implement the gospel, by means of floodlighting and spotlighting clarifying exemplification, so that people can have light on the issues for clarified living under our God.

11

Justification

Justification is the final step in the discussion of an issue, wherein we give reasons why we accept or reject what we define, elaborate, and exemplify, and determine why such an issue will be beneficial or detrimental to us in our thinking and living, so that we share with integrity the personal, decisional sense of the issue's relevance to us.

W HEN YOU JUSTIFY you are trying to get to what the thing means in itself. You can't apply it if you do not know what it means in and of itself. In all these processes we are getting down to one issue. You can't talk about justification unless you know what it is that you are trying to justify. The definition tells you *what it is.* The elaboration *spells out more specifically what it is* that you are talking about. The exemplification *shows you how it can operate.* The last question of justification is completely different, in that now that you know what this is all about, *Do you buy it?*

In order for you to justify your full position on the issue in your sermon, you need to do three things: (1) to begin with a personal *what-how-why* thesis of what your overall position is on the issue in a one-sentence statement; (2) to follow up on the clarification by cleaning up in a succeeding paragraph what would be the most problematic part of your personal thesis found in either the *what* or the *how* or the *why* part; and (3) to end up with an indication of how or when or where you will employ or use the issue in your ministry as a practical tool.

To exhibit how to carry out these three procedures in order to express your full position on the issue, let us suppose that I am try-ing to justify my full position on *the significance of definition as a*

tool for my ministry. Then I would carry out these three procedures in the following ways.

Now, the value of this issue of *definition* for me in my ministry
is that it makes me aware of something fundamental in communicating as a professional of the Word of God, in the sense of my
making sure that I always establish a comprehensive *what-mean-
ing* at the beginning of every discussion I engage in, so that I will
never again appear to be a complete idiot in discussing divine
issues on that preaching stage.

When I say that "I will never again appear to be a complete idiot
in discussing divine issues on that preaching stage," I am referring
to the fact that so many *preechahs* have fallacies floating in our
peanut-heads concerning what it really takes to help people grow
in Christ. And the basic error behind all those fallacies floating
around in so many *preechahs* dinny-dim-wit heads has to do with
the cockeyed notion that everything else but *meaning* in *preechin'*
is the divine fertilizer for helping people to grow in Christ.

And, as a consequence of this cockeyed notion swimming in so
many dinny-dim-wit heads, it is not surprising that we find so
many *preechahs* rehearsing and utilizing and bragging about their
special kind of gimmick without *meaning* in their *preechin'* to
move people to grow in Christ. Some brag about their developed
whoop that got the job done. Others brag about their special gravy
on the end that moved the folk. And many, many, many other
nitwits brag about many other kinds of gimmicks without *meaning* in their *preechin'* that is *buildin' de Kaingdom of GAWD* for
them.

Thus, with such fallacious ideas floating around in the steepled-
heads of so many *preechahs* who *clamb* their buncom-buncoms up
there on that preaching stage every Sunday, it should not be surprising that so few of us in the preaching workshop even think
about preaching definitions—since comprehensive meaning is so
low on the totem pole of what so many *preechahs* consider to be a
viable tool for helping people to grow in Christ. And, that is
exactly what I am referring to in my thesis when I say, "So that I
will never again appear to be a complete idiot in discussing divine
issues on that preaching stage."

Now, this issue of appearing to be a complete idiot *discussing* divine issues on that preaching stage is something that frightens me to death, because the meaningless disease is running rampant like an epidemic all over the place nowadays.

For instance, just choose any *chuich* at random, just flip a coin, or say eenie, meenie, minie, mo, choose any *chuich* at random, and you will more than likely run across a monkey who has *clambed* up on that stage trying to *preech* without a sermonic proposition, in 99 out of 100 instances, if it ain't 100 out of a 100 instances. In 99 to 100 out of 100 instances, you gon' run across a monkey up there on that stage trying to elaborate and trying to exemplify. And such efforts at elaborating and exemplifying gon' to be just like Melchizedek, born without a definitional mama or papa in 99 to 100 out of 100 instances. Many idiots up there do not realize that a proposition is the definition of the whole sermon, and you will find many idiots up there trying to *preech* without a sermonic proposition, in 99 to 100 out of 100 instances.

And that is exactly why so many people out there in those pews are often sitting up there batting their eyes kind-of-foolish-like, while we *is* driving home that clarifying elaboration and that powerful exemplification on a non-existent sermonic definition in *discussing* the issue on that stage. Frequently those people in those pews are baffled and confused and completely-in-the-dark about what it is by definition we are running our mouths about on that preaching stage, in 99 to 100 out of 100 instances.

Just check it out yourself!!! Flip a coin, or say eenie, meenie, minie, mo, and check it out at any *chuich* at random—yourself. And you will find that many people leave the *chuich* many-a-day unedified by the distinct absence of sermonic definitional meaning in our light chat from that stage. They live their lives many-a-year having heard no clear word from the Lord from that stage, since they cannot get a comprehensive grip on what we are trying to say in the name of the Lord by means of a sermonic definition, namely, a proposition.

And maybe, just maybe—such a lack of comprehensive *what*-meaning accounts for why so many people out there in those pews don't know a thing else to do for the Lord except to cut the f-o-o-o-l on them *bainches* in *chuich*, even after forty years of hearing our so-called *powvuhful soimons*. Cause if the jacklegs up there with a nasty collar on backwards ain't making no comprehensive sense, then what else, what else, what else are they suppose to do, except to find something to play with right there in *chuich* to entertain their b-o-r-e-d selves?

And what else, what else, what else is most convenient to start playing with right there in *chuich* than the precious name of J-E-E-E-S-U-S? They gon' definitely play with the precious name right there in *chuich*, due to lack of comprehensive meaning on what that precious name means by definition. Thus, we mislead others to become more idiotic in the so-called name of the Lord right there in *chuich* due to a lack of comprehensive, definitional-meaning about the name of Jesus. Yes, this is exactly what I am referring to in my thesis when I said, "so that I will never again appear to be a complete idiot in discussing divine issues on that preaching stage." Now, that is what developing an idea is all about.

12

Transitions

Transitions refer to the words, phrases, passages, and strategies of conveyance that we use in leading our hearers from one section to another in a given gospel proclamation. If we use appropriate indicators for turns, movements, and rest stops, the congregation can be in a position to follow along comprehending in a transfigurating way each part of the sermon, from beginning to end.

WE COME NOW TO A MAJOR ROCK that must be hurled by hand at Goliath the Giant, the sermonic body—*transitions*. Transitions relate not only to the body of the sermon, but also to every other element of the sermon. Since the body of the sermon requires transitional usage so much more than the other sermonic elements, I give *transitions* special attention in connection with the body of the sermon. For it is indeed easy for your hearers to be lost in transit in the massive body of the sermon.

Let me begin by defining the term *transition*—that is, get some meaning on the question of *what*. When you look at the term *transition* in terms of its root, you see the root *tra-* and *tran-*, both of which mean "to move something from one spot or time to another." For instance, you see the root *tra-* in such terms as "tra-de" (exchanging goods between persons or parties); "tra-dition" (communicating information and customs to subsequent generations); "tra-ffic" (the movement of vehicles and pedestrians, etc.). And of course there are myriads of *tran-* words, such as "tran-scend" (moving or dwelling above); "tran-scribe" (moving a copy to another sheet); "trans-form" (to change shape or mode of operation). Thus, in either sense, *tra-* or *tran-*, you see that the word *transition* has to do with "movement of some kind, change of some kind"—movement or change of ideas as it relates to the preaching discourse.

Now, I want you to be unmistakably clear about what I mean by *transition*, involving the movement of ideas. For when I say "movement," I do not mean "jumping" from one idea to another. To be sure, "jumping" is movement—that is movement of a kind. But the kind of movement, *transition*, that I have in mind here is graceful, orderly, smooth, connected movement.

In other words, I am referring to *transitions* as connecting bridges—not like "jumping" from one ravine to another, between which you will surely make people fall. But, rather, *transition* is like a connecting bridge. By connecting words and phrases and sentences, you take one idea to the very doorstep of another idea.

Now, this ability to take one idea to the doorstep of another is where I separate the adults from the children. For example, I can always tell when I am riding with a person "just learning to drive," because the car is forever jerking, jerking, jerking, about to snap my neck off. On the other hand, however, an experienced driver moves the car along smoothly.

And so it is in preaching. The jackleg "jumps" from one idea to the other without connectors. Even within a single paragraph, s/he will have you colliding head-on with an express train, since s/he would just as soon veer up some railroad tracks for a shortcut as drive down an expressway. It is always like riding cross-country over rock piles without tires and springs in a jackleg preacher's car. So riding with a jackleg is just like committing suicide.

But the expert, professional proclaimers of the Word of God drive on superhighways, through paved tunnels and over paved bridges in their sermonic cars. And they always warn their passengers when they are about to make a radical movement. Thus, the expert, professional proclaimer makes smooth, orderly, graceful, connected transitions in his/her sermonic car. Riding with them is just secure delight.

So, the *what* of our concern here has to do with smooth, orderly, graceful, connected movement, *transition* in your sermons— smooth movement from the time you present the text to the last word in the conclusion of your sermon. For in making the constructive movement in your sermonic delivery, you are bearing in mind the fourfold criteria—*ethos* (the welfare of your community of riders); *pathos* (compassion for your travelers); *logos* (the orderly, consistent being of your passengers); and *theos* (bringing your passengers face to face with their ultimate destination, which is their secure position). All of this has to do with making the sermon convenient for your hearers.

Now, let us move to the issue of the *why* of *transitions*. One reason for *transitions* has to do with the need for "turn indicators" on your sermonic cars—standard equipment on sermonic cars for indicating to pedestrians, other drivers, and our passengers when you are moving from one phase of a single idea to another phase of that same idea, such as in the introduction, or in the conclusion, or within a body point where a single idea is being discussed.

An example of moving from phase to phase on a single idea can be found in driving an automobile—where you move from one street to another, or from one lane to another, both requiring a right or left turn signal from either a "hand indication" or a mechanized turn-indicator. *Why?* You do this so that the public and our passengers will be informed of what you are doing or intend to do. No, you are not stopping; you are just turning corners or shifting lanes; and you will keep on moving toward your single objective. And, when these turn signals are properly given, other drivers can know what to do and won't be slamming on the brakes and blowing their horns at you, and cussing you out for reckless driving.

The same is so with turn indicators in your sermonic cars, when you are just turning corners or shifting lanes in moving—without stopping—toward your single-idea objective. For when you use proper connecting words, or phrases, or sentences to give turn-indication in driving a single idea to its destination, your hearers can know what to do and won't be slamming on brakes mentally and blowing their tops emotionally, and cussing you out for reckless preaching. So you need to give your congregation some kind of sermonic turn signal in order to be practicing safety first on the sermonic highway. Using the proper connectives as turn indicators is standard equipment on modern Master of Divinity cars, though

never-ever on jackleg cars—new or old. Turn indicators let your
hearers know when you are turning or shifting within the comple-
tion of presenting one sermonic idea.

Now, a second reason for *transitions* has to do with the need for
station indicators for your sermonic riders—standard procedure by
competent transportation agents in keeping their passengers
informed of their general location. Now, this kind of indication
applies specifically to the body of the sermon, where more than
one idea is being discussed—where more than one station stop
must be made before the journey is over.

Let me illustrate this station-indicating principle by supposing
that you are traveling by train from Boston to Atlanta. And let's
suppose that on the way to Atlanta you have three major stops—
New York, Philadelphia, and Washington, D.C. Now, let's suppose
that after leaving Boston you fall asleep for half an hour. How in
the world would you know where you are when you wake up,
whether you have passed New York or whether you are still on the
way to New York? So, all along the way to New York—the first leg
of the journey, the first major station stop, the conductor would be
reminding you that you are between Boston and the first point,
New York, by constantly referring to New York. And not only
would the conductor keep you reminded of New York on the way
to New York, but when you are coming into "New York! New
York! New York! New York!" That is what good train conductors
do—keep their passengers informed.

Even so, the preaching railroad companies need to be wise
enough, and considerate enough, to recognize that your passengers
need to be kept informed of their general location while traveling
between major points in the body of the sermon. So you too need
to provide some kind of sermonic conductors on your sermonic
trains. These conductors should be continuously referring to your
sermonic New York, and Philadelphia, and Washington, D.C.,
while you are in these sermonic body points.

Yes, indeed! Ain't no confusion about where you are when you
are riding between the introduction (Boston) and the conclusion
(Atlanta) on a competent "station proclaiming" conductor's train.
For within all of the station points, New York, Philadelphia, and

Washington, D.C., and at the end of all station points, the competent proclaiming conductor keeps the hearers-passengers well informed of where they are by continuously referring to that particular point in question—either directly by calling the point's name specifically, or indirectly by calling its synonym.

Now, this station calling is standard procedure for modern Master of Divinity proclaimers of the Word. But, of course, there are many jackleg-unproclaimers, who know nothing about where they themselves are at any point—that is, if they happen to have a point by accident—so everybody on their train travels at night at their own risk, with no lights on the train anywhere—not even on the engine heading down the track at ninety miles per hour.

A third reason for *transitions* has to do with the need for "rest stop indication"—the pause that refreshes the hearers by giving them a needed rest while riding with us on a long sermonic journey. For whether you realize it or not, when people are listening to you attentively, they are doing mental work from which they need rest. Knowing this need, competent preachers provide "rest stops" in their sermonic discourse—giving their hearers the "pause that refreshes," though not necessarily Coca-Cola.

For instance, just about everywhere nowadays, employers recognize the necessity of having coffee breaks—usually a ten-minute break in the morning, and the same thing in the afternoon. Employers realize that this ten-minute pause that refreshes is good for business. In fact, it has been proved time and time again that production has increased since the coffee break has been instituted in the business world—the holy pause in the business world is re-creative for better production and better employee morale.

Another example of a "rest stop" can be found in that same railroad trip from Boston to Atlanta. When the train pulls into New York, Philadelphia, and Washington, D.C., the conductor informs the passengers of how long the train will be there. So the passengers know that they have so many minutes to get off to get a newspaper, or some candy, or a cup of coffee in the station—even though they might not be getting off there permanently, for there are not only "station stops" but also "rest stops."

But even more than that, even when the train stops at

Nankipoo, and Tagipoo, and Stogipoo, these small junctions are "rest stops" too. To be sure, you can't get off the train to go into the station house to get coffee and candy and a newspaper unless you want to get left there, because the train doesn't stop there but a few minutes. But you can get up and stretch your legs without being jostled by a moving train. And you can go to the bathroom too, unjostled. So whether one is at a major station stop or merely at a small junction, both involve "rest stops."

Even so, the competent proclaimer also recognizes the need for having "rest stops" on his/her sermonic train. And you make this needed provision by having "temporal pauses" in your sermonic delivery—very short pauses of one beat between sentences; a longer pause of two to three beats between paragraphs; and very long pauses of five to seven beats between the six major elements of the sermon: *text, title, introduction, proposition, body,* and *conclusion,* and between the points in the body of the sermon. All these are places for "rest stops."

So maybe there is something significantly holy about the Sabbath Day—God taking a "rest stop" on the seventh day and commanding us to have "rest stops." For even though God might not have needed to rest, God knows that we are finite, tiring, wearying creatures, and he commanded that we take "holy pauses" for our refreshment and re-creation—commanding us to stop from our labors from time to time and rest.

Thus, like our Creator and Sustainer, the competent proclaimer is sympathetic with the finite hearers and deliberately commands the hearers to stop and rest from listening by pausing in the sermon. For you are aware that the minds of your listeners are following your train of thought "on the run." So you must pause from time to time in order for them to catch up with you and get their breath back, before starting out again. That is what the modern Master of Divinity proclaimer does.

But of course you know that this is not so with the jackleg unproclaimer. Jacklegs think that the congregation is trying to get ahead of them in the race (and, sorry to say, the congregation is usually ahead of jacklegs in every way). So out of their inferiority complex (and inferiority is a reality because with jacklegs it is not just a complex), they strike a trot at the text, gain momentum at the title, and break into a run down the highway like a bat out of hell through the "Amen" at the end of their introduction. Now, I said "through their 'Amen' at the end of their introduction," because you and I both know that they never heard of a proposition and that they never have any body points, except the one maybe on their steeple heads.

We are now coming into Atlanta, folks. Rest stop indication— giving your beloved hearers the needed pause that refreshes, so that your preaching can be for your congregation like the eternal Sunday in the eschaton with our God.

13

Substance and Form in Proclaiming a Relevant Gospel

Substance refers to the essential content of the issue being discussed, which is always designated by nouns/pronouns that give a name to the subject matter for understanding what Theos, ethos, pathos, and logos mean in terms of the issue's basic nature.

Form refers to the operational context of the issue being discussed, which is always designated by verbs giving assertion to the issue, for understanding how Theos, ethos, pathos, and logos function in the issue's basic mode of operation.

LIFE APPEARS IN THE UNION of substance and form. All life, everything we know, comes in some organic substantial form. Genesis says that God, the Creator, called for light (form) in the midst of the existing chaos (substance) in the very beginning—the evening and the morning being the first substantial day formed. *Substance* means being sure that we have the right content or material or stuff or meaning of the gospel, in terms of presenting the spiritual medicine needed by our sin-sick hearers, so that they can be getting well from the prescriptions put down from the pulpit. *Form* means being sure that we employ the right method or manner or way for presenting the gospel substance, in terms of using the right kind of procedure to get the spiritual medicine into the spiritual systems of our sin-sick hearers more efficiently, so that they can be getting well easier by the way we put the prescription down from the pulpit. A creative union of substance and form is needed in individual, marital, pastoral, social, and international relations, as well as in preaching for being well off under our God.

Now, let us wrestle with the meaning and biblical application of this whole business of substance and form in proclaiming a relevant gospel, by using the definition of four Greek words that can aid us in gaining more insight and winning more victories on this issue—namely, the Greek terms *Theos, ethos, pathos,* and *logos,* which can be like images in a mirror darkly, for us in the dark to see more clearly what our God would have us to do in God's name in these hellish times of our.

THEOS

Theos, in general, is that which is considered to be of ultimate concern for people's being and well-being, to which they give absolute devotion. *Theos* is the deity, divine, absolute, God of ultimate devotion. The key ideas in this literal meaning are *ultimate* and *absolute* which indicate the supreme significance attached to what people consider accounting for the good, the beautiful, and the true in life. Every era in history gives evidence of belief in some kind of Supreme Being in every culture. Even *cullud* folk hanging out on the *cornah* have a belief in some kind of supreme being, to which they give ultimate and absolute devotion, whether we recognize it or not. One *cullud* person's trinity is something like this: "some greenbacks being God the Father making things happen for you; some liquor being God the Holy Ghost making you feel good inside; *de women(ses)* being God the Son in *de* flesh *brainging* joy to *de* world." The evidence of this *cullud* person's belief is that he will *preech* a sermon on *airy* one of these three things, plus get happy and shout on that *cornah* about these three Gods of *his(n)*.

However, Christian *Theos* that is relevant to proclaiming the gospel, in spirit, involves always talking about being genuinely committed to *Theos* for our being and well-being, that is, always talking deep soul-talk from the pulpit. Anything less than deep soul-talk from the pulpit is a pure waste of people's time—not worth nothing whether done in church or in the streets. Anything less than deep soul-talk produces hypocrites in our local churches, who lack the power of the spirit to do the will of *Theos,* such as those nice things we bid them do without giving divine reasons to the soul for doing those nice things. In essence, *Theos*-spirit empowers the soul to do good inwardly, by means of proclaiming *Theos*-reason in depth for people to be born again of *Theos* in the soul.

In addition, proclaiming the gospel in truth involves always telling that which is genuinely correct about *Theos*, that is, according to what the Lord has taught us about *Theos* from the pulpits. Far too often, black proclaimers are most irrelevant in reference to *Theos*, far too often saying something old and nothing new, something borrowed from a fool that ain't never true. Another negative implication is the possibility of leading black folk to worship idols with enthusiasm every Lord's Day, meaning that we could be leading people straight to hell from the pulpit. *Theos*-in-truth means that black folk will be getting some genuine blessing from the true and living *Theos*, so that they can be free and liberated indeed under the banner of the true *Theos*. The Psalmist says: "Blessed is that nation [or race or people] who's *Theos* is the Holy One of Israel."

The following are specific suggestions on *Theos* resources. The New Testament tester/correcter on *Theos* discussed above—in spirit and in truth—comes from John 4:21-24. Romans 1:19-20 says that the will of *Theos* can be known, since it is revealed in everything around us. Matthew 5:43-48 tells us what *Theos* is like in relation to those against Jesus. Matthew 6:5-34 describes ways of *Theos* in reference to prayer, religious piety, fasting, our daily allegiance, and our daily needs. Luke 15:1-32 is a parable about *Theos*'s attitude toward sinners saved, which is often mis-preached on sheep-raising, penny-finding, and family-life, but is really about *Theos* rejoicing when those against *Theos* return. John 3:16 is *Theos* loving the world, not just the church, as the reason for all that has been done by *Theos* in what the Bible is talking about. The whole Bible is saying something about *Theos* primarily, even though it seems in places to be centered on some person or thing as the occasion for talking about the ways of *Theos*. Hebrews 11:1–12:3 gives us this holistic picture. We need to use the whole Bible for preaching texts, since it is all about the transmission of the Word of God as redemptive and reconciling power.

ETHOS

The literal meaning of *ethos* refers to the character or interest or sentiment or loyalty or disposition of a community of people, embracing something in common as their community bond or rallying theme, for the purpose of individual and mutual well-being of the whole community. The term *eth-os* has the same root implications as the terms *eth-nic* and *eth-nos*—with both these other terms referring also to certain common traits of the group binding them into a fellowship or kindred minds with power.

An example of *ethos*-power is found in the children of Israel being bound together by their common experience in the name of Jehovah, with Jewish people today and the prophets of old—"Hear, O Israel, the Lord Our God is One Lord"—appealing to that *ethos*-principle mightily for nearly four thousand years in Jewish history.

Another example can be found in emphases on black power, black agendas, and black-black as means of binding blacks together into a possible fellowship with kindred minds with power. Now this is only potential *ethos* because there is no automatic *ethos*-principle in merely having common black skin.

The relation of *ethics* to *ethos* is like that of Siamese twins. *Ethics* has to do with appropriate communal attitudes and conduct and behavior, expressed by those who live together in close proximity in the group, for the progress and protection and well-being of all in the community—with the community insisting that everybody in the group be trained and abide by the meaning of the moral principles established for the group, unless we want to end up with nothing. With all the immoral cancers being spread in our communities unchecked, ethics is desperately needed. There is no other alternative for us, if we want to stop ending up with nothing. *Ethics* in our relevant proclamation is one means for helping black folks to remove that immoral ball and chain still hanging around our necks enslaving us inwardly.

Specific examples of resources for *ethos* can be found in the whole Epistle of James, wherein the concern is not so much with intellectual and professing elements of faith, but with day-to-day living of it. Both of Timothy's epistles are excellent on ministerial ethics at all levels (annual conferences, ordinations, installations, and institutes). The book of Deuteronomy is the moral codebook for ethical living in the Old Testament. Exodus 20:1-17 contains the Ten Commandments, which have almost been forgotten in these times and need to be updated for solving problems today. In toto, *ethos* requires that we relate the Word of God to the particular problems and needs of the congregation.

PATHOS

The literal meaning of *pathos* has to do with having pity on someone; feeling what another is going through; getting into another person's shoes. The root relatives of *pathos* are such terms as *com-pas-sion* (com = with; pas = feeling); *sym-path-y* (sym = with; path = feeling); *em-path-y* (em = involved; path = feeling). *Pathos* has to do with understanding and using the other person's common language (experience) when trying to get the Lord's heavenly meaning over, so that the other person can get God's meaning at his/her gut-feeling level.

Our heavenly Father became incarnate, in order to speak to us on earth at our human gut-feeling level. Jesus Christ taught us through parables, in order to speak to us at our experiential gut-feeling level. Matthew 13:34 indicates that Jesus always taught in parables, and without a parable he taught nothing. Jesus spoke financial parables to business people, familial parables to mamas and daddies, agricultural parables to farmers, pastoral parables to shepherds, and so on. A parable is an exemplary type of communication device, whereby one teaches something unknown by means of relating that something unknown to something commonly known, so that things known will throw light on and inform about things unknown. In these lectures I have used gut-level words such as low-down and *doity, cullud* folks, nasty-collar on backwards, doo-doo, etc., all deliberately designed to speak to your living gut-feelings. In fact, the expression "Ho-hum" should not rise in worship, if our hearers hear the gospel in a known tongue.

The basis for *pathos* is found in the nature of man and woman, who are basically emotional beings as well as rational and deciding beings. The basis of the Great Commandment is the primary order to love God with all our mind (thinking), soul (deciding) and heart (feelings). And in our preaching, people need to be led to abhor the devil's ways and to pine after God's ways at the gut-feeling level. The whole chapter of Matthew 23 presents Jesus in rare form. Jesus uses *pathos* expressions to denounce the ways of phony religious leaders of his day. In Matthew 16:23-24 Jesus uses *pathos* expressions to rebuke one of his best friends, Peter, when Peter got out of hand.

LOGOS

The urgency of *logos* consideration in our proclaiming a relevant gospel is based on our strong emphasis on *pathos*, which could mislead you into thinking that yours truly has gone hog-wild about feeling in religion like so many other *cullud* folks. *Logos* in general has to do with people's need to be making rational judgments about the truth and meaning of what is being heard and experienced, so that they can make reasonable decisions for living it.

Logos in particular involves the *logic of being* and the *logic of consistency*. The *logic of being* is the concern for making sure that our proclamation is related to factual reality, so that people can see the connection between the gospel proclaimed and what is happening in real life, since fairy tales can be told logically too. The question "Is it so?" should not be present in worship.

The *logic of consistency* involves both jiving and orderly statements in proclaiming the gospel. Consistent jiving statements have to do with making sure that what we say at one time/place is in harmony (agreement) with what we say at every other time/place in our proclaiming. In other words, all of our statements should be compatible with each other, since the appearance of lying is worse than the appearance of stealing in terms of killing a preacher's influence with the folk. The consistent order of statements has to do with making sure that what we say is designed in proper sequence from beginning to end of our proclaiming, so that people will not get lost in trying to follow the discourse. Our statements should flow with ease. *Preechahs* misleading folk *dat-a-way*, with disorganized procedure, necd to be B-A-M-M-E-D on their peanut-heads with a logical blackjack, so that they can have some kind of logical point, even if it means a knot on their steeple-heads from a logical blackjack.

Suggestive patterns of logical spatial order would be right to left, left to right, up to down, or down to up, or in to out, or out to in, in terms of the way it exists in space. Logical temporal order moves from earlier to later, or later to earlier in terms of the way things happen in time (never middle to beginning to end). Logical qualitative order deals with worse to better or better to worse. And logical quantitative order moves from smaller to larger or larger to smaller.

Let's look again at the logical order and logical reason for designing discussional parts of sermons: Introduction (heart-feeling), Body Points (mind-thinking) and Conclusion (soul-deciding). The question, "Where is the preacher?" should not arise in worship, because people can follow railroad tracks but not a maze. You must go about getting logical content for every part of your sermons.

SOME COMMON ERRORS IN THE BODY OF THE SERMON

Fallacies of Criterion

1. *Lecturism.* Where *ethos* and *pathos* are omitted and the sermon becomes a presentation of a term paper or dissertation to the congregation. They want this truth, but not straight from the classroom.

2. *Alogosianism.* Where one has no regard for planned sequence and presents the body points as if the diamond design is a universal order for all sermons.

3. *Sandism.* Where one has an interesting, logical oration which leaves people happy and informed, but far from redemption. I remember one preacher who preached on the theme that a dead lion is less powerful than a living dog. We all enjoyed it, but so did we enjoy balling the night before.

Material Fallacies

1. *Divisional nominalism.* Where one confuses a subdivision with being the second body point and/or confuses a second point with being a subdivision of the first point. Now these kinds of people confuse themselves with the deity. They think that because they say it is point 1, it has to be point 1, regardless of the content. They spake it and it is done.

2. *Twenty-minuteism.* Where one is more concerned with clock watching than with doing a thorough job in explicating an idea. The idea here is to be out of church at 12:25, not to carry the congregation into the heights and depths of the unsearchable riches of Christ. It is little wonder that the people begin to look at the clock too; they have a good example to follow.

3. *Hide-and-go-seekism.* Where preachers foolishly try to hide their sermonic divisions from the congregation to show their artistic ability in sermon delivery. There is no better way to put a congregation to sleep than through this foolish method of trying to lose them deliberately.

4. *Illustrating-the-illustrationism.* Where one uses an unclear illustration which itself is in need of clarification. It is as if one uses a burned-out light bulb in a dark room and then lights a candle to show that s/he has a light in the room.

Formal Fallacies

1. *Blind-guidism.* Where one tries to construct a sermonic body without the aid of numerical or topical propositions and/or a rough outline. It is like trying to build the Empire State Building out of jelly. The more one tries to build, the more messy it becomes.

2. *Successism.* Where one has preached a good sermon accidentally, according to one design, and feels that the design is a holy instrument in all his/her sermonizing. Design should be related to the content to be dealt with, plus the aim of the sermon. Such preachers who would use the same blueprint

to build a dog house and a cathedral, just because they built a nice dog house once upon a time, should have to live in the dog house as far as congregations are concerned.

Argumentative Fallacies

1. *Biblicism.* Where one uses the Bible as the alpha and omega of his/her argument by quoting Scriptures throughout the discourse. The text itself is enough Scripture for the sermon and should be explicated and argued on other grounds. More unexplicated texts merely make the task more difficult for the congregation to be convinced.

2. *Argumentism.* Where one endeavors to prove that which is obvious to everybody concerned. Carrying a known truth to a deeper dimension of understanding is one thing; but arguing about whether Jesus had twelve disciples is quite unnecessary. Argumentation is a tool to get a task done and should not be used to display the intellectual genius of the preacher. Most people know that we have an M.Div.

3. *One-trackism.* Where one has felt successful in the use of a particular kind of argument and feels that this kind of argument will win every argumentative battle. This is the weakest position that one can hold, because any enemy can prepare an offensive against a traditional fortress.

14

Procedures in the Conclusion of the Sermon

The conclusion is the last formal rhetorical element in our homiletical process, wherein our concern is to lead the congregation to a decision about the clarified issue, since preaching by its very nature of edification and evangelism calls for either a "Yea, Lord" or a "Nay, Lord," but never a "Maybe, Lord."

THE *CONCLUSION* IS THE MEANS for bringing our hearers face-to-face with God, bringing to a head all that we have said thus far in other parts of the sermon, so that people can be led to think and feel and do and be something new and different and holy under God through our sermon. Those other sermonic elements, *text, title, introduction, proposition,* and *body* are not ends in themselves, but are means to the end of leading our hearers to the goal of ultimate response to God in the *conclusion* of the sermon.

Therefore, what shall we say about this all-important, final, rhetorical element, whose major concern is with ultimate end and divine response? What can we say here about this weighty matter of preaching law, which stands at the very omega of all our proclaiming effort? Well, in response to those weighty questions about divine preaching law, let us say three things about the *conclusion* of the sermon, at least a word in terms of those dialogical questions about *what* and *why* and *how* of sermonic conclusions.

The literal meaning of *conclusion* is the prefix *con-* meaning "with" and the root *clus-* meaning "closed" or "shut off," with the whole term meaning the way in which something is closed or shut off meaningfully. Some of the root relatives of *clus-* are *in-clus-ion,* meaning to "close or shut something in"; *ex-clus-ion*, meaning "to close or shut something out"; and *pre-clus-ion*, meaning "to exclude something at the beginning." A literal sermonic meaning of *conclusion* means the closing or shutting off of the sermon so as to elicit a response.

Sophisticated synonyms of *conclusion*, expressions meaning the same thing, include: climax, consequence, consummation, decision, destination, determination, effect, end, finale, goal, judgment, the last, objective, omega, purpose, result, summation, ultimate, eschaton. More common synonyms include: touchdown, home run, swish of the net, T.K.O or knockout, bingo, the Oscar or Emmy Award, the *winnah*, the prize, bedtime children, good night or good-bye, pay day, my "A" or my "F" in the course, my M.Div. degree, my certificate, what it all adds up to.

The ultimate meaning of life itself is to come into the full presence of our heavenly Father, by deciding in the soul to cherish God's laws for creative living under our God. A symbolic football summary is that we will not settle for less than a touchdown as our ultimate aim in preaching, with not even a field goal being satisfactory. Touchdown! Touchdown! We want nothing less than a touchdown!!!

The *why* of the *conclusion* is that there are always two overall objectives in every sermon, known as *evangelism* and *edification* (called "Old Ev" and "Old Edi" for short), if we are aiming at preaching touchdowns all the time. Now, *evangelism* ("Old Ev") means gearing our sermons always to the increase of God's kingdom, quantitatively, in order to extend God's rule to include other people for the first time. Nominal members who are merely on the rolls of the local church need to be offered Christ all the time. Nicodemus-type leaders, those merely on the top rungs of the church, need to be born again for the first time. In other words, we need to open the doors of the church at the end of every sermon to offer Christ to little devils and big devils inside and outside the church, since the evangelical victory for our God is far from won in the world.

Edification ("Old Edi") means gearing our sermons always to the increase of God's kingdom, qualitatively, in order to develop God's people inside the church. One of the problems in the black pulpit is the fact of predominantly uneducated ministers, which reflects inadequate church leadership. Another is the black pew problem, which is the consequence of untrained leadership, with pews being filled with religious pigmies having said they felt something forty years ago, but still being as stupid in the Lord now as they were before starting to hop them *bainches* forty years ago. In summary, we need to open up the doors of the church during every sermon, by offering something new about Christ for those religious runts to grow up in Christ inside the church, since they often need some fertilizer at the root of their faith to grow toward perfection in God.

The general procedure of *how* to conclude is based on whether the spiritual problem in the *sermonic introduction* is either a problem of the mind (thinking) or of the heart (feeling or doing) or of the soul (deciding)—all three of which relate to the first and great commandment in loving our God.

The specific procedure of a *thinking conclusion* involves the edification of the mind, which can be done by stimulating thought in two ways, for helping to love God better in our thinking. One way is *recapitulation,* reminding our hearers of the essence of the body points by repeating the essence of each point, in order for the mind to recall them. An example is the way we ended the discussion above on "Old Ev" and "Old Edi." The other way to do a *thinking conclusion* is *resume. Resume* is adding up the meaning of the body points, not by repeating them, but by giving the sum total implication of the body points all together, for the mind to get their implicative meaning. The writer of Ecclesiastes uses a *resume* in his conclusion. After wrestling with all the vanity of vanities in the book, the writer says at last, now, this is the conclusion of the whole matter. "Fear God and keep all of the commandments, for that is the whole duty of man." Another example of *resume* is Apostle Paul's conclusion in 1 Corinthian 13, "and the greatest of these is love."

A *doing/acting conclusion* involves the stirring up of emotions, by giving them a specific assignment to get busy with, for helping to love God better in our functioning. The two principles to remember about sermonic assignments: (a) being sure it is something that all can do; and (b) being sure that it is related to something suggested in one of the body points.

A *being/deciding conclusion* involves challenge to the soul, which is done in ways to invite the soul to decision, for helping to love God better in our deciding. The *living option way* places alternatives before the soul, in terms of the negative (Introduction Problem) and the positive (Body Solution) to decide which way to go. Like Joshua, we ask, Which God will you serve? The *directive way* places an order before the soul, in terms of suggesting the positive only, for making the soul aware that there is only one, real alternative. Like Joshua, we say, "As for me and my house . . ." A *living option/directive combination* is a final way to do *being/deciding conclusions*.

SOME RESPONSIVE OBJECTIVES SOUGHT

The response sought will determine not only the kind of *conclusion* employed, but also the *introduction*, the *proposition*, and the *body*. We can only hit that which we aim at deliberately. While such suggested responses do not exhaust the manifold nature of human responses, they do have in mind the trichotomous nature of human beings, involving *knowing*, *feeling*, and *willing*.

1. *God-felt sorrow* or *repentance.* Genuinely knowing that sin is real, and that it abounds within and without the congregation, and that such response is a positive ingredient for renewed fellowship with God must be the constant objective in preaching. In fact I doubt seriously whether we can be imitators of the teaching of Jesus without the "Repent! For the Kingdom of heaven is at hand."

2. *Conversion.* Knowing that the world is not redeemed—in fact, knowing that our churches are not redeemed—leaves this objective open to us always. While the objective of repentance could very well apply to both Christians and non-Christians, this has in mind specifically the non-Christians.

3. *Edification.* This concerns the deeper meanings and implications of the gospel. Ignorance and mental laziness will

always be with us as long as the world is, especially concerning the deeper meanings and implications of the Christian faith. Few laypeople think through the meaning of their
faith or love God with all their minds without assistance.
Many are still living with the elementary concepts and fruits
of the Spirit.

4. *Growing edge of concern.* While this is closely related to
   edification, I am concerned here with the more practical
   expression of edification. For example, we know that we
   must love all people, but we do not always know just how we
   can express that love to others.

5. *Sympathy.* This means feeling what others and what God
   must feel. Here the emphasis is upon identifying love,
   putting ourselves in the place of another who is suffering,
   hoping, laboring, paining.

6. *Concrete action.* Since we know that "Faith without works
   is dead," there are times when we want our congregations to
   do something concrete in the kingdom. It might be picket-
   ing, or sending a supply of food to the hungry, or petitioning
   the government, or the like.

7. *Spiritual curiosity.* In a multifarious kingdom, where God
   calls each to work in the kingdom according to his/her
   unique capacities, it is not always possible to suggest a specific response. We must leave the congregation at the throne
   of grace, looking unto God for the specific orders for their
   lives.

8. *Renewal* and *regeneration.* In a world full of human sin,
   bred from the very inception of human history, to be sure,
   there is constant need for lifting burdened people to new
   dimensions of power and refreshment. All of us constantly
   need the refreshing view of Jesus and his Word, because life
   is unpitiably cruel.

9. *Sense of human dignity.* No greater problem is manifest in
   our times than the sense of human insignificance. Dwarfed

by shackles of racism, super colossal doom staring at us, the impersonalism of contemporary societal forces, we would despair if we were not assured that we are "somebody" and that God does love us.

10. *Jubilation.* One of the ingrained needs of the human soul is to stand in the presence of the good, the beautiful, and the true in adoration. One of the chief ends of humanity, if not the chief, is to adore God. In the midst of all that is not God, the incarnation of the glory and grace of God can take place once again in the sermon.

There are many more objectives. If we were to try to list them all, I am sure we would not be able to finish this discussion.

COMMON ERRORS INVOLVING CONCLUSIONS

1. *Unholy spiritism.* When the preacher does not plan a conclusion but relies on the Holy Spirit in that hour. The false intention here is to leave room for God in the sermon. Three fallacies lie in this view of the conclusion:

   a. The Holy Spirit should be involved throughout the sermon. If not, then it is doubtful whether the Spirit will feel welcomed at the last minute. In fact, God should be involved in the very beginning of the service.

   b. The Holy Spirit is both omnipresent and eternal. The Spirit is in the study closet as well as in the so-called holy place, the sanctuary. The Spirit is either with us seven days per week or not at all; if the message is holy by the time you get it to the pulpit, it is very likely that your sermon will be hallowed in the conclusion.

   c. Most of us are not good "cuff" speakers, because we have to watch our grammar as well as our content. I imagine this fallacy causes many of us to saunter into some of the other fallacies described below, because nothing comes at the end of our sermons.

2. *Immediate actionism* happens in sermonic conclusions for many of us because we know that we should evoke some kind of response, and, in turn, we feel that the response must be evident to prove that the congregation is actually responding. Thus, we try to get the people to buck-dance and tear-up-the-church on the spot. The true response will begin in worship, but it will carry over into life. It might be years before we see the true fruits of a sermon. Nevertheless, so many numbskulls confuse worship with service. They try to use up the people's energy in a forest fire inside the church. The only thing left for the congregation to do is go home, take a bath, and go to bed, because "they have had it." They have been to the "service."

3. *Noisism* takes place whenever preachers confuse a powerful sermonic conclusion with the volume of noise that the lungs can produce at this juncture.

4. *Weeping emotionalism* is the kind of sermonic conclusion wherein the preacher confuses "bringing tears to their eyes" with the full meaning of response. The preachers save emotion-packed words like "JESUS!" and "MOTHER!" to scream at the end.

5. *Displayism.* Preachers try to convince the congregation every Sunday that they have not lost their power to be eloquent. If such preachers could forget about this, maybe, just maybe, Jesus could get to the congregation.

6. *False agape-ism.* The preacher feels that all sermons should end on a sentimental note, disregarding the reality of the need for repentance. To be sure, we cannot minimize the grace of God, but such does not negate the seriousness of God.

7. *Uniconclusionism.* Jacklegs end all sermons the same way, irrespective of what has been discussed before. At this point in the sermon the youth prepare to fidget and the elderly wake up.

8. *Exasperationism.* Jacklegs indicate with such words as "finally," "in conclusion," and so on, to show that they are

coming to the end of the sermon, rather than through more artistic means. Usually the jackleg has lost them after the first sentence of the introduction, so maybe using the word "finally" might be an act of kindness. However, there is a more excellent way to be kind.

9. *Poemism.* Poetic quotations become the only way for some preachers to conclude a sermon. In our seminary days, we ridiculed a bad sermon with the expression, "He had his usual three points and a poem." While this is not intended to suggest that poetic conclusions should be outlawed, it is intended to suggest that some poems should not be over used.

10. *Buckshotism.* Jacklegs either raise other or new issues in the conclusion and/or do not boil the sermon down to one specific issue. Here the people are confused in two ways: (a) they do not understand fully the meaning of the new idea because it has not been clarified in the previous discussion; or (b) the congregation is confused as to which issue to commit themselves to because two issues are being sold. Unanimity of understanding and of issues is mandatory in making a sale.

11. *Cadet pilotism.* The preacher circles and circles the field for minutes because s/he has not planned how or where to land. Such jacklegs swoop low, and we as listeners feel that they are landing, but jacklegs take off again for another try.

12. *Compound summary.* All—and I do mean *all*—of the above errors have one thing in common, namely, that they take the minds of the people away from the issue to something else. If we don't have many sales, or if people do buy (as some do when they come down the aisle to join these churches), it is basically the work of God *in spite* of the jacklegs.

SOME TYPES OF CONCLUSIONS

The list given below is merely suggestive, not exhaustive. The type of conclusion employed will depend largely upon your responsive objectives.

1. *Recapitulation* or *resume.* This is the recollection of the main streams of the sermon in a final, synoptic view. Care must be used in this type of conclusion, because great art is needed here. It is not merely announcing the main points of the sermon. Rather, it consists in a compounding of these main streams with the elements of force and persuasion. "And now abideth faith, hope, and love; these three, but the greatest of these is love." "And what doth the Lord require of thee, but to live justly, to love mercy, and to walk humbly before Thy God." "And this is the conclusion of the whole matter; fear God and keep His commandments."

2. *Direct appeal.* This is tied closely to the concern for conversion. "Come unto me all ye that are heavily laden. . . ."

3. *Directive.* Tell the congregation exactly what you want them to do. For example, at the Annual Conference I suggested that we veterans of the ordination experience use the ordination service as an experience of repentance for the mess that we have made of God's kingdom; for in genuine repentance, the kingdom of heaven will come nearer than our doorsteps.

4. *Christian answer to the big question.* Particularly where the whole sermonic discourse has been of a problem-raising nature, the answer is found in the conclusion. "What shall I render unto the Lord, my God, for all his benefits unto me?" The answer is "restoration of the self completely."

5. *Subtle or open dare.* A challenge for the congregation to put their faith on the line, though sometimes needed, can be a dangerous kind of activity.

6. *Dramatic portrayal.* A decisively revealing event is paraded before the eyes of the congregation, a portrayal that in itself evokes the response needed. The parables of Jesus indicate the power of suggestion in narration.

7. *Open-ended question.* One merely raises the ultimate questions, questions to which the answer is known but must be fulfilled in the individual members of the congregation.

"Knowing what all of this means, do you still want to preach?"

8. *Wooer's note.* The minister plays the part of John Alden in proposing for Miles Standish. If our best lover can be won through expressions of "sweet nothing," so can the congregation be made to fall in love with God.

SOME POINTERS ON CONSTRUCTING CONCLUSIONS

1. *Definitive objective.* This should be in mind at the very beginning of the sermon. Personally, I suggest that the conclusion be written as the first item of the sermon after a proposition is in view. My reasoning behind this is that a person ought to know where one is going before one begins to travel. This does not mean that the conclusion might not be rewritten for polish and greater effectiveness; but the sermon ought to "buy a ticket for some destination" before jumping on a train at random. Some homilists disagree with this emphasis, but all of us do agree that a destination should at least be clearly in mind at the very beginning. A subject always implies an object toward which it is directed; a proposition, likewise, implies some particular claim upon its hearers.

2. *Tedious Laboring on Construction*
   a. *Whole conclusion.* Sins are allowable, though not encouraged, in other places in the sermon; but perfection is absolutely necessary in the conclusion. Write it, rewrite it, and rewrite it until the conclusion is a work of art. Practice the conclusion, practice it, and repractice it until you know your conclusion by heart. Live with your conclusion: eat it, sleep with it until the conclusion is something that you feel with conviction. Then you will appear before the congregation with an illumined countenance (like Moses), and the people will respond because they will know that you have been with the Lord.

b. *Specific part.* Labor should be given to the last sentence in the sermon. This sentence should be the most impressive sentence in your discourse. It ought to arrest, impress, and provoke response. Speaking in a business sense, this is the clincher.

3. *Brevity* is essential to a conclusion. Thus, mastery of words is essential. Conciseness, however, must not mitigate the precise end sought. Each word must be chosen carefully, so that it can carry absolutely its own weight. The conclusion should be not more than 10 percent of the sermon's length.

15

Anatomy of the Idea

An Exemplary Discussion for the Ear

The anatomy of the idea has to do with grasping the full thrust of an issue being discussed, by means of raising certain kinds of basic comprehending questions about what is being said or written, with a view toward understanding what the issue means-in-itself and what it implies-for-the-audience.

SINCE THE ANATOMY OF THE IDEA is a most important concept in meaningful communication, I will use this concept as the substance of our endeavor to clarify a few matters. I will make sure that I am repeating the essence of each part of that definition each time, in order for the ear to get it.

AN EXAMPLE OF ELABORATING THAT DEFINITION FOR THE EAR

What we are saying here means that we are concerned with being put in the know fully about something to gain insight into the meaning and the relevance of ideas, which is accomplished by putting to ideas functional questions for meaning. Answering relevant questions for comprehending ideas and their implications is germane to being genuinely informed on the issues.

In other words, being in the know fully about something involves having answers to basic questions about the meaning and significance of things. All in all, we are saying here that the *anatomy of the idea* means getting full comprehension through basic questioning for being edified on what the issue stands for per se and what the issue suggests for creative living. [Please note that

I can put the *what-how-why* in any order I choose, so long as I am accurate about its meaning and include all the parts in each restatement of the original definition.]

What are the kinds of comprehending questions that relate to meaning in itself and to implications for the audience? Well, let us begin with the kinds of comprehending questions that relate to meaning in itself—which H. Grady Davis (*Design for Preaching*) refers to as structural questions. The structural questions for basic meaning are these: *what* is being talked about (basic substance) and *how* that something is being talked about (basic form).

The first kind of structural question relative to basic substance has to do with comprehending *what* that whole issue is all about— so that we can understand the basic subject of the entire discourse. If one does not understand the basic subject, then no other question would be relevant until that *what-mystery* is solved at the get-go. The second kind of structural question relative to basic form has to do with comprehending *how* that whole issue will be dealt with—so that we understand the basic assertion of the entire discourse. Because if we do not understand the basic assertion, then a *how-mystery* emerges on the scene as a ghost to haunt us the rest of the way. Thus, those first two structural questions have to do with raising some basic *what* and *how* questions about that entire discussion—so that one can make a clear determination about *what* that whole discourse means in itself, and about *how* that whole discourse can be followed in a meaningful way.

Now after, not before, but after one comprehends *what* and *how* that whole issue is being discussed in terms of its basic meaning and procedure from a structural stance, then one is in a position to raise other kinds of relevant questions in terms of its implications for the audience, which Davis refers to as functional questions. A discourse is not relevant only in terms of what it means in itself, but takes on significance only in terms of understanding what it implies for me in my creative living, functionally.

The three functional questions Davis sets forth regarding the validity and value and relevance of the discourse for the audience are these: Is it true? What difference does it make? Do I believe it? In essence, these functional kinds of questions have to do with the basic *why* question about an issue for justificational purposes about my life and its living meaning.

Thus, what Davis, as our textbook authority, is talking about in his chapter on the Anatomy of the Idea is closely related to what Clark, your teacher, has been endeavoring to drive home in setting forth definition, elaboration, exemplification, and justification for conveying meaning and implications in creative discussion. Those structural and functional questions in that chapter have to do with the sharing and reception of meaning and implications in a comprehensive way—just as those four stages of discussion have to do with that self-same objective of receiving and sharing of meaning and implications in a detailed way.

Special Note: There is no way—absolutely no way—to exemplify issues in our preaching without relating that issue to something concrete. And, because we are always discussing some aspect of preaching in all that we do in this class, it is mandatory—absolutely mandatory—that what we choose to work on must be related to preaching. In a word, it is impossible to exemplify issues in this preaching class without making up an imaginary preaching subject or some kind of preaching issue to show how that issue would work in a preaching situation.

For instance, if you are exemplifying an issue in a biblical or historical or theological class, you would need to choose something biblical, historical, or theological connected to the issue in order to be relevant in those other classes. Likewise, in no way—in absolutely no way—can you be exemplifying the issues in this preaching class on such things as boats and cars and trains and planes and food and drink and sex and pleasure—except parabolically. Thus, you must exemplify something on preaching in your preaching assignments in order to show *how* it would work relevantly in preaching.

AN EXAMPLE OF EXEMPLIFICATION
ON THE ANATOMY OF THE IDEA

Now, *how* does this issue of the *anatomy of the idea* relate to preaching or communication in a concrete way? Let me relate this issue to preaching and communication by using it in a sermon entitled "I and IT," on which I will raise basic structural and functional questions about that subject to get at its meaning and implications.

For example, let me raise structural question number 1 about that subject: *What* am I talking about? Well, the subject "I and It" is talking about finding (the "I" part) and losing (the "It" part) oneself in the midst of life's pressures and temptations. That is *what* that subject is talking about.

Again, for example, let me raise structural question number 2 about that subject: *How* am I talking about it? Well, the subject "I and It" (finding and losing oneself) is being talked about from a twofold temporal perspective: (1) from the temporal perspective of young folk just starting out in life facing all kinds of temptations prompting them to lose themselves relative to their ultimate objectives under God; and (2) from the temporal perspective of old folk having been out there in life already beaten by all kinds of temptations and having lost themselves relative to their ultimate objectives under God. That is *how* that subject is being talked about.

Still again, for example, let me raise a functional question about that subject: *Why* am I talking about it that way? Well, the subject "I and It" (finding and losing oneself) is being talked about that way because it involves the most important game of life for everybody—whether old or young—because it involves the most precious thing to me, namely, self. That is *why* that subject is being talked about that way.

Thus, with answers to those basic questions of meaning about that subject, I am now in position to work out the details of that subject in a sermon in a meaningful way—simply because I have worked out the *anatomy of the idea* on that subject and know the basic meaning of the *what* and *how* and *why* of it, comprehensively.

AN EXAMPLE OF JUSTIFICATION ON ANATOMY OF THE IDEA

Why is this issue of the *anatomy of the idea* significant for me? Well, this issue is significant because . . . it will do *what* in some specific *way* for some significant *reason*. The justification is always personal in your preaching.

16

Four Bitter Pills for Black Revolutionary Religion

Four bitter pills for revolutionary religion bear witness to Clark's last will and testament to professionals of the Word of God to always have something of supreme value for our hearers' contemporary well-being in each and every sermon. Anything less is a waste of time. Anything other than gratitude, repentance, a black religious revolution in Jesus' name, and a renewed commitment to preaching as holy intellectual inquiry will only help people become religious hypocrites with no power in the depths of their being to know that Jesus is calling us to faithful living, morning by morning, day by day

A MOST IMPORTANT QUESTION is whether or not it is at all possible for us to overcome, since we are all aware of the heavy weight of historical sin making us desperately sick, especially after what we have been through in history. We know that we, as a people, are desperately sick with spiritual cancer in our souls. And thus, I raise the question as to whether or not there is a doctor in the house. Is there a doctor in this place for some sin-sick souls born in agony yesterday?

And by accident, or by divine providence, there happens to be a doctor in the house. And the doctor recommends four bitter pills that we need to take every day from now on, if we are to overcome this malignant spiritual cancer in our souls, wherein generation after generation we are being infected by it. And we will take those bitter pills today.

Now, one of those bitter pills has to do with our need to be grateful to our God for helping us to survive as a race by means of our good-for-nothing religion of the past. Our old-time religion was good for nothing, but God blessed us with it. In spite of the fact that our religion wasn't nothing at all to work with, our God blessed us with the ability to survive as a race by means of it, even against Mister Charlie and his endeavor to make us good chattel slaves with that good-for-nothing religion.

And thus, we black people need to thank our God from the depths of our souls that we had that good-for-nothing religion, since a lot of indigenous people are just about extinct now as a race because they did not have our kind of race-surviving religion. They tried to defend themselves against a majority of whites with those bows and arrows, while the whites had rifles and shotguns. It was sure defeat—lying out there with a bow and an arrow, trying to stretch it back as their only weapon of defense. You can't whip no majority by physical means. I don't care how black your butt is. You can't whip the white majority by physical means so you might as well forget that. You see what happened to the Black Panthers who were trying to get armament together to whip a white major- ity. And, they too are just about now extinct. A minority can't whip a majority in terms of physical means.

You whip the majority by having spiritual power. That is how Martin Luther King, Jr., got the Voting Rights Act passed and the Housing Rights Act passed and the New Civil Rights Bill passed. Not with guns but with soul power. That is what we need to sur- vive and to prosper against a majority that wants to oppress us. Soul Power!

So the first bitter pill has to do with gratitude. We need to be grateful. Some of us are ashamed of our old-time religion but there is no need to be ashamed of it. That is all we had. That good-for- nothing old-time religion is all we had. We ain't had nothing but that. Now, it wasn't nothing, but it was all that we had. And God got a blessing out of it for us. And we don't have to be ashamed of what we had in the past, in no sense of the term. So the first bitter pill has to do with gratitude for the obvious blessing of old-time religion from our God, for it helped our race to survive in a desper- ate situation.

Now, the second bitter pill that we must take has to do with our need for repenting under our God for trying to use this inadequate religion from the past in our present stride toward freedom. We are looking for better things in the present, but at the same time we are worshiping the idol gods of those funkmakers and hog callers of Mr. Charlie in that religion behind the big white house of slavery. And thus we black people need to sit in sackcloth and ashes. We need to fall down on our knees before our God in repentance for still trying to worship those idol gods of the past in much of present-day black religion.

Much of our religion smells from that manure of the past. So we ought to be on our knees in repentance to God for carrying that sack of manure too long into the present. We need to repent for not taking a stand against jacklegs right here in our midst who are rehearsing that old funkmaking in preparation for perpetuating that same good-for-nothing religion in the pews in today's black church. Someone need to kick his or her ass for rehearsing that funkmaking in the black church, today. The only way to repent is to let the Lord know that you resent jackleggism every time you hear it.

So that second bitter pill has to do with repentance for the obvious sin of making peace, making peace with funkmakers and hog callers in our midst who are working against the true and living God. Instead, we need to kick their ass and run their ass out of this community. We need to let them know that they ain't welcome. It is the only way that we can repent for trying to use inadequate religion from the past in our present situation.

And that goes for theologically trained seminarians who act like jacklegs behind that sacred desk. Y'all need to deal with that yourselves. Deal with jacklegs in the class cheating on you and then end up being on the honor roll. You ought to kick the jackleg's ass. Always talk to them first. It might be that they need a sermon or so, and they might repent and be saved. So don't kick their ass right away. But if those funkmakers start acting crazy and acting like they don't understand what you are talking about, then get a delegation, not no one person tackling them, get about six or seven per delegation and kick their ass. And threaten them, that if you ever again act like jacklegs, you will expose them to the authorities, so that they can throw their ass out of this community, because we don't go for that.

Now, a third bitter pill has to do with our need to have a

religious revolution in the name of our Lord, by means of grounding our religion on a solid biblical foundation in the interest of living according to some religious truth. We need to shovel all of that old-time religious poop, along with all of those *cullud*, funkmaking jacklegs off the black religious scene, by latching on to nothing less than what our homeboy, Jesus Christ, really stood for ages ago. That is how we do it. We commit ourselves to something that is genuine, and that means automatically that something that is faulty is out of the way and off the scene.

As a very eminent scholar says, "The Black religious drama is not going well and no mere shifting of scenery on the Black stage will fix the drama." We need some new black actors in the play. We need new black people who are born again and changed by the power of Christ in a revolutionary way. We cannot simply use the same, dumb, sinful actors anymore. We need a black religious revolution in Jesus' name. We need a completely new black religion in Jesus' name. We need to construct something completely new rather than repairing something old from the past. We need a black religious revolution with a new foundation laid in Jesus Christ, and nothing but Jesus Christ.

Funkmakers are always coming around telling you what you need. Young man, you need to go downtown and buy yourself some new suits if you want to be successful. You need to get a delegation of young folks to go to these old funkmakers. Some of you think that they have influence because they are old, gray, and looking prosperous. And, you think that they know something. And you, young whipper-snapper seminarians end up getting sucked into their funkmaking. Yes, we need to get a young delegation to deal with idiots like that. Talk to them first, but you know they ain't going to hear you. Kick their old, gray-headed funkmaking ass.

Let me see it. Invite me to the party. And when they go back to the authorities and say Dr. Clark . . . I will say that you weren't even there, because you were in my class at that time. Yes sir, I would tell a lie on something like that. Hell, yeah! I just hate funkmakers. I just hate that kind of stuff.

So, we are referring here to a new religion, with a new name on it, not that old funkmaking, hog-calling stuff, but a new religion with a new name on it, led by new leaders like you and me, for a new people under an ever-renewing God, who alone can save us in this new revolutionary age of ours. So, the third bitter pill has to do with a black religious revolution in Jesus' name, for the construction of something new and relevant and helpful for black people to really overcome in the name of the Lord.

And now, we come to take a fourth and final bitter, bitter pill by which we hope that you can really overcome in Jesus' name. Those other three pills can help you relieve the pain in your cancerous souls, but they cannot actually cure the pain in your souls. They can give you some relief. They can give you help but they cannot cure the cancer. Only the fourth bitter pill can really cure the cancer in your souls. So let's get to that fourth bitter pill for some real healing in your souls.

Now, even still further, in the fourth place, you must bear in mind that your overcoming has to do with your need to be committed. I didn't say hop no benches. You must be committed in body and soul for the fulfillment of this new way under our God, even if it involves a cross for you. Every new creation, every new creation must, under necessity, involve blood and sweat and tears by means of bearing a cross for fulfillment. Without the shedding of blood, without somebody's living blood being shed, without the shedding of blood, there can never be the removal of sin, as the biblical writers wisely informed us about life.

Ain't no use in talking about removing no sin without somebody dying to remove that sin. It is a bitter pill, isn't it? Thus, it is the cross, wrapped around resurrection. The cross is the central theme for black Christian living in these times of striving for black liberation. Some folks are talking about the cross being inferior to the resurrection when the cross is the most important part of the gospel. Why do you think that they put crosses on spires and not an empty tomb? Crosses at the top of churches? And crosses on the communion table? Nobody goes in there and say that we are going to have a celebration and a sacrament for the resurrection, but it is in remembrance of the death and passion that we come once a month to celebrate something that is most important for our Christian living. So, you better get your theology straight. It is the cross and not the resurrection that is the central theme for black Christian living in these times of striving for black liberation.

It is the cross that must symbolize our identification with and our dedication to our homeboy, Jesus Christ, by making a supreme sacrifice for a new black religion, with some real black power in it, for some genuine liberation and reconciliation under our God in Jesus' name. The only way that the revolution is going to come is by shouldering up a cross. This is the bitter pill that we are talking about here.

And believe me, you better believe me, that it is indeed a heavy cross, and often a double-cross. This is what we are trying to say here about our commitment to something new in our religion. Many black people themselves are deeply infected by the cancerous disease of the old slave religion. And black people will try to block your progress as a new leader among them, even to the point of trying to kill you when you try to promote the new way under our God in Jesus' name. So you need to keep in the center of your mind what I said about that vaccination of religious toxin that Mr. Charlie put in our forefathers' religious veins that took, and it is still taking even now.

Thus, your biggest cross, or your biggest double-cross will probably involve black folks themselves as Moses found out, and as Jesus found out, and as every other revolutionary in history found out, as they came to their own race of people who received them not. That is the tragedy of human history. You try to go back and help your folk and they go to fighting you. It ain't the enemy that is the problem; it is when your own folk go to fighting you.

Moses went back to Egypt. He didn't want to go. He was a prince in the house of Pharaoh. He had all the privileges of affluence. He could have stayed there. He gave that up and joined with the minority in slavery. And that is the group that he had the most trouble with. All those plagues that Moses put on Pharaoh's butt wasn't nothing. His biggest problem was with those folks going across that desert. They almost killed Moses crossing that desert. That is why when Moses came down off that mountain and saw those fools down there funkmaking, and he has just gotten the message from God, he got to cussing and burst the tablets with the commandments on them. Moses was trying to help somebody and they were down there fighting him.

You know it was true with Jesus. Your own people will be the ones to break your heart and will crucify you on the cross. So don't fool yourself as to who the enemy is. We ain't saying that other folks are not a problem. But we are saying that your primary problem ain't in other butts. Your biggest problem in the black church community is with black butts. That is where you will experience your real cross and your double-cross. It is going to be a double-cross when you try to help your own people.

Now, this issue of bearing the cross for something new is also what the Hebrew writer was dramatizing as he concluded the 11th chapter of Hebrews. Remember that? And Moses did this, and so and so did this, and the people of faith fought lions, and conquered kingdoms, and so on, but they all died in faith not seeing the fruit of their labor.

And we too might have to die in faith, as did all the saints of old. None of them received the reality of a new age in their lifetime that they worked so hard to produce. You must also work and preach as if that new age is here already, just as they had to work. For like them, we will also see merely the beams of the sun on the distant hills of the dawning of a new day. We won't see the sun itself. We will merely see the beams, the rays of the sun on the distant hill coming forth. And that is all we will ever see of what we are trying to get done. And we too must die before the full morning sun rises above those distant hills; we must also believe in our hearts that morning always comes, because God has promised that morning shall follow night, and we know that.

Even though we do not see that full sun rising, we work with the promise of God knowing that morning always comes. That is the way that all saints and revolutionaries must work—with the assuring promise of God that morning always comes, with or without us. And that is why we work in faith, not seeing the promise of God, but believing in God that if I plant my life, if I plant a seed in your soil, something is going to happen. God is going to see that it happens, because morning always comes after the night. The sun is always rising and setting. It never fails. And it tells me something about God. Just as that sun never fails, God never fails. Morning always comes.

So in the light of that assuring promise, let me make it clear, that I, your teacher (let me do some testifying this morning), do here and now commit myself to you only, in terms of a new way of teaching you. I don't have to look around and see what no funkmakers have to tell me about teaching. I am committed to the new way—a unique way, my way under God, in teaching you. You need to know that my mind is made up and my heart is fixed to work with you only in terms of something new in your preaching, under God. Even if it involves a cross for me, even if I must die without having seen the promise of God come to fruition in my lifetime, in terms of what I am trying to teach you. I believe that somehow when I am dead the next generation will have a new breed of preachers. I know that the jacklegs are in predominance now. But I know that just like the sun rises and sets every day, that morning in my ministry always comes with or without me.

And let me also inform you that yours truly has not just begun to think in terms of the new way. I have been thinking about something new for black folks long before the revolutionary movement began in the 1950s and the 1960s and 1970s. So don't think that you are ahead of me for being a revolutionary. You are way behind me in being a revolutionary, because I was a revolutionary when it wasn't popular in terms of doing something new. This stranger has been converted to this new way ever since he began teaching nappy heads like yours in 1955 to be somebody worthwhile as informed and dedicated prophets, nearly twenty years now. I have been at this business of trying to get some dedicated and some informed people to be the new breed in the church. So you ain't dealing with no Johnny-come-lately in this black revolutionary business in Jesus' name.

Thus, now that you have some idea of where this stranger stands, are you all with me on this? You need to hear this because I have some questions to put to everybody here. Let me ask you some disquieting questions about where you stand as most of you make your first turn at the corner in coming from behind the big white house of slavery.

Let me ask you this, what are you concerned about, really? I don't mean just what you mouthed, but what are you really concerned about? What do you live for? Ultimately? And what will you die for, if you have to? Why did you really turn your nasty collar around backwards in the first place? For a big church? Or for a new age dawning in the life of black folks? For a big name for yourself? Or for a new being in yourself? For crowds following you and applauding you? Or for congregations following our Lord Jesus Christ to victory? What do you believe in deeply in your soul, is what I want to know. Why did you really turn your nasty collar around backwards? I raise these kinds of disquieting questions for you to think about deeply and for you to decide about deeply in your soul, when you talk about commitment, as you make your first turn at the corner, coming from behind the big white house of slavery. Let me ask you this because I need to know this: ARE YOU INTERESTED IN SOMETHING NEW FOR BLACK FOLKS? Would you mind working hard in this preaching endeavor? I would like to know that.

Now to those, and only to those, I ain't talking to nobody else, but to those who are committed, to those who are really interested in working hard, because that is the only way that we are going to work on your sermon preparation and delivery, let me inform you that we are now about to get a new show on the road. A new ball game is about to begin. The curtain of the old show is now falling. The ninth inning of the old ball game has been played. And now, now we are about to commence something that is completely new in black preaching. And the name of this new thing being commenced is called black homiletics. The concept of black homiletics is all about the new way to proclaim a renewing gospel, in a new age, for creating new people, for a renewing God, for some genuine liberation under our God, in Jesus' name.

So let us set forth a holy proposition on this renewing concept for some genuine liberation in our preaching, because we desperately need to be liberated from a long, dark night of racial oppression, and exploitation, and cutting the fool on them benches over nothing but bell ringing, with no gospel food presented by those *cullud* hog callers on that preaching stage. And nothing but a holy proposition on something new can save us from all of that. And that holy liberating proposition is the following:

Therefore, in the light of our ultimate concern to make all things new, through a religious revolution, and in the light of our ultimate concern to be involved in the promotion of a new creation, personally, let us wrestle non-stop with this holy concept, *homiletics, in two significant ways. Now, you know **what** we are going to do, don't you? You know **how** we are going to do it (in two significant ways), and **why** are we going to deal with it in two significant ways (to usher in a new age).* We need a new age.

We are merely reiterating the *how* here. One way is to define precisely what we mean by the term homiletics, in general, at the get-go. And then, second, to spell out in detail what we mean by the term *black homiletics* in terms of six homiletical parts of a sermon, in particular (*text, title, introduction, proposition, body points, and conclusion*) throughout the rest of the discursive part of this course of study. You got the whole idea there in that proposition, haven't you? You know *what* we are going to do, *how* we are going to do it, and *why* we are doing it.

And that is all that you are going to be working on for the rest of your preaching life, black homiletics, in two significant ways.